*Guideposts
to Creative
Family
Worship*

Guideposts to Creative Family Worship

**ANNA LAURA and
EDWARD W. GEBHARD**

ABINGDON PRESS
New York   *Nashville*

GUIDEPOSTS TO CREATIVE FAMILY WORSHIP

Copyright MCMLIII by Pierce & Washabaugh

Library of Congress Catalog Card Number: 53-6350

Scripture quotations, unless otherwise noted,
are from the Revised Standard Version
of the Bible and are copyright 1946
1952 by Division of Christian Education
of the National Council of the Churches
of Christ in the United States of America.

The lines on page 89 from *The Prophet*
by Kahlil Gibran are used by permission
of Alfred A. Knopf, Inc. Copyright 1923
by Kahlil Gibran, renewal copyright
1951 by Administrators C.T.A. of Kahlil
Gibran Estate and Mary Gibran.

SET UP, PRINTED, AND BOUND BY THE
PARTHENON PRESS, AT NASHVILLE,
TENNESSEE, UNITED STATES OF AMERICA

To Our Parents

Harry and Vera Munro
and
Gabriel and Paulina Gebhard

who shared with their children
their own firm faith in God
by living it

CONTENTS

Guideposts
to Creative
Family
Worship

Roots of Family Religion

SOME TIME AGO IN A MIDWEST NEWSPAPER THERE appeared the picture of a court scene in which one young man was testifying against another. The defendant, charged with fraud, was being tried for gambling with funds which had been entrusted to him. One fact loomed in the testimony: both young men had faced the same temptation. One had held steady and the other had weakened. What had made the difference?

A superficial analysis showed that both boys came from comfortable middle-class homes of churchgoing parents. Closer observation revealed, however, that one family had consistently lived the faith it professed on Sunday. But the only religion the other home really knew was that of outward forms which had been sloughed off as useless by their growing son. He had adopted the secular standards of the soda-fountain set. Father and son both enjoyed a little gambling and an occasional drink. And when the "get-rich-quick" scheme was suggested to the boy, he was an easy mark.

The court found him guilty and sentenced him to prison. The moral laxity of the one young man, the moral integrity of the other—what had made the difference?

A young couple asked their minister, "What makes the difference in marriages? With so many marriages ending in the divorce court, how can we safeguard our home?"

Every home has its times of crisis. Every family faces its periods of sorrow and its experiences of tension. But some come through their times of testing with stronger loyalties and love for one another. Such families have found a living faith that sustains and upholds them, not only in times of difficulty, but through every day as well.

The main root of their sustaining faith is a uniting loyalty to something greater than themselves—a loyalty to God. They know they are children of a loving Father. Differences of opinion may arise among them, but differences of spirit will not, for the ultimate values by which they measure life are rooted in their loyalty to the Supreme Good.

And so they recognize God in the daily round of life. They show him the same courtesies they extend to their friends. They include him in their conversation around the table. They seek to understand his viewpoint. They seek his counsel in hours of decision and share with him their joys in times of triumph. God will not intrude. He is able to sustain and strengthen and bless their home far beyond their understanding, but they must open the door.

The family of faith recognizes God's presence in its midst and comes to experience the sustaining power of his fellowship. Prayer for that family is not so much a formal practice set aside from the requisites of the day as it is a natural and abiding companionship with the Presence. With the prophet of old the family of faith has discovered, "If with all your heart ye truly seek Me, ye shall surely ever find Me."

Moreover, the Christian family finds in the Bible, particularly in the teachings of Jesus, a guide and a resource for daily living. The family with a vital faith discovers that the Bible is a record of "man's unceasing quest for God and God's unceasing quest for man," which puts it far on the highway toward a rewarding experience of God.

Finally, a family of faith participates in the fellowship of Christians, the Church. In the Church its members find an incentive for personal growth and an outlet for fellowship and service. The Christian family does not build walls around itself to keep out the distractions and evils of the world. Rather, it has the qualities of salt—it preserves not itself, but the good in its environment; it adds zest and flavor to the life around it; it has antiseptic healing qualities that restore the open sores of society to health. And Christian families discover in their union with one another a redemptive fellowship which is extensive and outgoing.

Here, then, are the roots of an enduring faith that holds a home firm. And all these roots—recognizing the presence of God, cultivating prayer, appreciating and using the Bible, and participating in the fellowship of other Christians—are found in the truly Christian home. These make the difference between direction and frustration, between a sense of belonging and insecurity, and between faith and fear.

Moreover, these are the elements that have always characterized Christian families. Jesus spoke of yeast, which when hidden in dough raises the whole lump, giving it a new quality, a new taste, and a new appearance. The Christian families in the first century did exactly that in their culture. The early churches had their beginnings in such homes. Paul speaks of "the church that is in their house," and we picture a family unit bound together by a firm faith in Christ's way, reaching out to redeem its pagan environment through the power of Christian love.

One way in which Martin Luther gave expression to his

protesting revolt was by establishing a Christian home. Then he gave the Bible to thousands of other German families in a language which they could understand so that its resources were available for their needs.

Methodism's founder was born in the Epworth rectory, where an inspired mother hid the leaven of spiritual truth in the minds of her children. And the moral fiber of our nation was wrought in thousands of pioneer homes where the presence of God was daily acknowledged, where prayer was a sustaining and strengthening force, where the Bible was frequently the only textbook, and where circuit-riding preachers often led the way into new territories, planting steeples across the prairies.

But something has happened to American life. The weeds of little loyalties and the dry rot of moral decay have moved in to choke out the plant that bears the fruits of the spirit.

Jesus, too, lived in a time of crisis. His nation was a defeated people familiar with the fruits of bitterness and oppression. Government had become an unbearable yoke, and clouds of hopelessness engulfed his nation. The refuge of his people was their homes, and the religious heritage was treasured and shared there. In the desperate history of the Jewish people their organized religion has been driven underground many times. But as long as there are Jewish homes the faith continues.

Jesus must have known such a home. For the great religious thought of his people, the tried and tested resources for living wrought out by generations of seeking after God, bubbles from his speech so naturally that it is hard to say, "This is from his heritage; that is his own matchless insight."

Jesus saw the Nazareth home through the eyes of creative insight. His great, out-going spirit saw all life in terms of the basic values which he experienced at home. The most meaningful term ever found to express the outreaching love of God is Jesus' familiar and loving name "Father." And Jesus felt himself brother not only to James and Joses and Simon, but to all whose need challenged his sympathy, and he called all men "brothers." Moreover, the power in which he put his trust, the power he earnestly believed to be the strongest in all the world, the power upon which he depended to build the Kingdom of God, is the self-same power which gives birth to a family, and then nurtures and sustains it. It is the power of love. Truly, Jesus' concept of the Kingdom of God, about which he taught with such directness and winsomeness, is really a family of God, in which God is the recognized Father of all men. More than one hundred times in his teachings Jesus used these familiar family words to explain his meaning.

And so the Christian family has a particular responsibility in its society. For it is really the primary unit of the Kingdom of God—it is the Kingdom in microcosm.

If you could go to the Master, as mothers long ago went seeking his blessing for their little children, and as fathers went to him begging him to heal the sickness of their sons—if you could go to him and ask, "Master, what must I do?" he would say to you as he said to them, "Have faith"—that living faith rooted in love for God, in the religious heritage, in prayer, and in fellowship with your brothers.

For Jesus saw religious practices as an expression of the heart that loved God. Jesus did not discard the religious forms of his day, even though they were inadequate for his message. He read the scriptures, he practiced prayer, he worshiped with his fellow men in the synagogues. He recognized in the formal practices of religion, as set forth in the Law and the Prophets,

vessels of the spirit. He criticized them because they were so
often empty, devoid of the values they should be treasuring.

Jesus would not therefore destroy the vessel. "Do not think,"
he said, "that I have come to destroy the Law and the Prophets.
I have not come to destroy them, but to fulfill them"—
literally, to fill them to the full. And so he said, "Yes, love your
neighbors as you have been taught to, but don't stop with that.
Love your enemies too, and prove yourselves true sons of your
Father." So full did he fill the symbols of men that he made of
the disgraceful cross a symbol of redeeming love.

And what of our religious practices? Is the keeping of them
the way to possess and maintain our Christian faith? Many
families have discarded the forms of religion—regular reading
of the Scriptures, grace before meals, family prayers, regular
church attendance in the family pew, family discipline that
governs action—because they have become empty. They were
all right for a slower and less exciting day, but where does
one find time for them now? And what is the attraction in
them?

These are the questions the modern family asks, until suddenly it discovers that it has lost a vital faith which will sustain
in periods of crisis, and which will put joy and purpose into
every day. Then it seeks methods of family religion—natural
and meaningful methods—that will nourish the parched and
dying roots of its faith.

Here, then, in this book are forms and methods of family
worship which some families have found growing, flowering,
and fruiting from a vital Christian faith. No family will find
all of them useful for its needs, nor will it find the same method
of value at all times. Take them and use those that have value
to you now. Next year your needs may be different and other
forms may have meaning for those needs.

Have you ever stood before a forest of trees stripped bare of their leaves by the ravages of insects? After three or four years of infestation many of the trees themselves will die, for the roots alone cannot nourish a tree. The living tree is equally dependent upon the outspreading leaves. The chlorophyll in the leaves, through the process of photosynthesis, transforms the energy of the sun into nourishment for the leaves, the branches, the trunk, and the roots.

Likewise, a living faith is dependent upon vital religious practices. They are the spiritual chlorophyll which transforms the radiant spirit of God into wholeness of life and spirit.

Growing Toward God

YOUR CHILD IN THE HIGH CHAIR AND THE EARNEST builder of blocks on the living-room carpet may be the most profound theologians in your home. At least your little children are asking the most far-reaching questions about life that they will ever ask. And they are getting answers too—answers that you may be giving quite unknowingly.

Before a child begins the first grade, he has asked, and has had answered, the basic queries of life. Few of his questions have been phrased into words. By inarticulate ways he asks the first question, "Who am I?"

Have you ever watched with delight the fascination of a tiny baby who discovers his own fingers or toes? Grasping in the air at random he touches something—something that responds with feeling. He loses it and tries again, this time with purpose. For several minutes he plays with his fingers and toes—wide eyes full of the wonder of discovery.

During the weeks and months when a baby is getting acquainted with himself, the parents who surround him with warm, responsive love are saying to him in the only language that he can understand, "You are a person, you are wanted and loved, you have value, and we care for you." And long before a child can grasp a mental concept of his own worth, he experiences the love which surrounds him—and he feels secure. As he

18

grows older and phrases his answers in theological language, he may say, "Every person is of supreme worth because he is a child of God. We are surrounded by the loving concern of our Father." But his first step toward understanding and experiencing God comes in babyhood.

The second question, "Who are you?" is asked by the infant almost as early as the first. And if he could phrase his feelings into words, he might say, "You satisfy my needs. I know your voice. I feel your hands. You are a person and I can trust your care. I can respond to you with love, and you need me just as I need you."

In this first response of a little child to another person the basis of all social relationships is laid. His first outreach toward another is that reaching for his mother, then his father, and other family members. The kind of interaction he experiences with his family in the inarticulate days of his infancy will lay the foundations for the social attitudes and skills he expresses later.

When he matures enough to put into words the reality he experienced from early babyhood, he may say, "Love your neighbor as you do yourself, and treat other people as you would like to have them treat you." Whether these Christian concepts can hold real meaning for him may depend upon how his family helped him answer the question, "Who are you?"

The next question that faces a little child is the query, "How am I different?" The toddler begins to explore himself in comparison with other persons and other things. He is soon aware of the functions of the various parts of his body, and he discovers that he is different from the persons and things around him.

"Jack can run faster than I can, but I can jump down more stairs," Billy tells his mother. Merry Gail learns she can win a place by flashing a winsome smile, while sister Carol is the songbird of the family.

The basic discovery the little child makes in answer to "How am I different?" is, "No one else is quite like me. I have a special place all my own in the family and in the world." Initiative or withdrawal, self-respect or lack of confidence, may be the result of the answers to this question.

In later years, the child may read this scripture with understanding: "Now there are varieties of gifts, but the same Spirit; and there are varieties of service, but the same Lord; and there are varieties of working, but it is the same God who inspires them all in every one. To each is given the manifestation of the Spirit for the common good." (I Cor. 12:4-7 R.S.V.)

The most important questions of all which the little child asks over and over again are: "Why? Why am I? Why are you?" And in answer to the question "Why?" the whole meaning and purpose of life itself is involved. No parent can answer it satisfactorily for his child unless he has found the girdings of a strong religious faith. And if he has that faith and lives by it, the halting words he may use to answer his child's persistent gropings will not matter much. The child will discover the answer in the attitudes expressed at home, in the things that matter to his parents, in the loyalties that bind his family to one another, to the world, and to God.

He will go on seeking through childhood and youth the answer to "Why?" and it will not be answered satisfactorily until he becomes a contributive, self-giving personality who has found a worthy purpose for his life. Just as the responses you give to the tiny baby's physical needs for food, comfort, and warmth determine his physical wholeness and health, so the answers you give to his quests for meanings determine his psychological and spiritual wholeness.

The little child asking persistently "Who?" "How?" "Why?" is not far from worship. Wonder, not duty, is the beginning of worship. Parents who want their children to grow in love toward God and others will learn to use these spontaneous openings for worship. For our children's wonderings and questings are really thermometers to their religious growth. And our ability to recognize them is a rather accurate thermometer of our own spiritual sensitivity.

Here, then, are some doorways through which we can expect the spontaneous sort of responses that lead to worship.

1. Experiences with nature may make lasting impressions upon children. As a parent, you can help make those experiences both beautiful and meaningful by carefully explaining that God, as the Creator of all things, has a purpose and a use for all nature's wonders. The purple fringes of a gloxinia blossom opened in our home one day, and the plant was placed upon the table.

"How long do you think it took for that flower to grow?" Daddy questioned the family.

"Well, how long did it?" the children asked.

"Three years ago we planted a tiny seed. We tended and watered it, and placed it where it would get a little sunshine, but not too much. Then the leaves grew strong and green, and a healthy bulb grew in the pot. And now, after three years, we have a flower."

"Why, it's older than me," said the youngest. There was a moment of quiet as we studied the flower.

"What does that teach us about God?" Mother finally said.

One of the children answered, "Sometimes he takes an awfully long time to make something beautiful, and sometimes we have to wait."

How naturally the scripture followed, "He hath made everything beautiful in its time."

A family who faced a far-reaching decision often paused together to watch their pair of canaries which were nesting. They saw the mother bird build her nest in the basket strainer. They noticed how the father bird fed her and sang to her as she sat upon the nest. Then one afternoon as the family gathered about the birds, their mother voiced the wonder they all felt.

"When we see God's laws at work in his tiny feathered creatures, how can we doubt that they are at work in the hearts and minds of men."

Perhaps the eleven-year-old did not understand all that her mother meant, but she answered, "That sounds like something Jesus said about birds, Mother. Find it in the Bible."

And so the mother turned to Luke 12:24 and read: "Consider the ravens: they neither sow nor reap, they have neither store house nor barn, and yet God feeds them. Of how much more value are you than the birds!"

Stepping from the door of wonder into the room of worship, the mother had shared with her family her faith in the forces of the Eternal.

2. The persistent questions and remarks of our children are like the slits of a partly opened door into young minds. Through them we can glimpse their wonderings and concerns, and sometimes find ourselves upon the threshold of worship.

Every Thursday noon was question time in the Jones household. For ten-year-old Billy the wonderings stimulated by the news stories in the fifth-grade *Weekly Reader* were never fully satisfied at school. Once it was a story about the size and habits of whales which set off a train of questions and reactions that filled the noontime with excited chatter.

"I'll bring the paper home tonight, Mom, so you and Dad can learn about whales too," he promised.

The supper conversation was a mixture of football and whales. And when the supper dishes were cleared and the tall candles were lit, Billy's father turned to the first chapter of Genesis and read some verses from the great poem of creation.

And God said, Let the waters bring forth abundantly the moving creatures that hath life, and fowl that may fly above the earth in the open firmament of heaven.

And God created great whales, and every living creature that moveth, which the waters brought forth abundantly, after their kind, and every winged fowl after his kind: and God saw that it was good.

He concluded simply with the remark, "You see, Billy, even whales are a part of God's great plan."

3. Experiences of appreciating people, of enjoying friendships, and of participating in activities of sharing provide another doorway into worship.

The five-year-old who came home from kindergarten and began setting the lunch table to the singing of "Jesus Went About Doing Good" was not far from worship.

One day when a neighbor came to help the family during a period of illness, five-year-old Nancy remarked, "After Mrs. Albright leaves, it feels just as though Jesus had been here." Perhaps Nancy was more sensitive to spiritual values then her mother, who had accepted the neighbor's gesture as an expected courtesy.

4. Occasionally in the solving of conflicts or problems experiences of worship will emerge.

When eight-year-old Sam and six-year-old Ben moved into a

new community, they were beset by a neighborhood group of youngsters their own age who opened persistent warfare upon all their play. Having a great desire to make friends, the newcomers were in no mood for counterattack. One day when a one-sided battle of mudballs was in session, Sam sought out his mother.

"I can't see why all the kids around here think they have to fight all the time," he said.

"Well, Sam," she replied, "they're probably just trying to get acquainted."

"They've got a mighty silly way of making friends," Sam said.

"Maybe you can show them a better way."

An idea struck him. "Say, Mom, what about those cookies you made this morning—and some lemonade? Do you think that would work?"

"You might try it," his mother answered. "I'll make the lemonade; then you and Ben can call a truce."

Half an hour later the mud-spattered porch was the scene of a laughing peace parley.

"Why didn't you kids fight back?" asked the tallest of the neighbors.

"We know a better way of getting acquainted than that," Sam said, with his mouth full of cookies.

"I'll say you do," another youngster agreed as he reached for the last cookie on the plate.

That night at bedtime Ben remarked, "The kids around here are really nice when they stop fighting and start playing. Why did they fight us anyway?"

"People often fight what they don't know," their mother remarked. "You boys just put a more important rule to work— a rule that Jesus gave men a long time ago about returning good for evil."

A few minutes later one of the boys prayed, "Thank you, God, for showing us a happy way to make friends and be friends."

What should parents do when the spontaneous questions and experiences of their children lead to holy ground? Long ago Job was told, "Stand still, think of the wonders of God" (Moffatt).

1. Wonder with your children! The parents who pause to wonder with them say, perhaps not in words, but in actions which children can understand better than they do words: "The mysteries of God are important. We trust in the evidences of his care and have faith in what is beyond our understanding."

2. Sometimes it will seem natural to express your feelings in words—to define the experience. This is what the parents in the family who watched the gloxinia bloom attempted to do. And it is what the mother, who found an answer to her own needs in observing the nesting canaries, tried to share with her family.

Sometimes the child will define the experience as the little girl did when she sensed the good will of her neighbor's help. The only responsibility the parent has then is to accept and recognize the truth a child has observed. An appropriate prayer thought or verse of scripture will often heighten the impression of the experience.

3. At other times the experience may be defined by a resolve. One sunny morning, after enjoying a hearty breakfast, the family had an exuberant feeling of well-being, and impulsively expressed it with merry laughter. Impressed, the eldest child remarked with a note of wistfulness in her voice, "Let's be like this all day. Let's keep it sunny."

But remember, the definition does not produce the worship

experience. It only heightens the impression of the moment upon us, and gives us a handle by which we can recall it and later use it.

4. Frequently we will want to recall and highlight these spontaneous experiences in formal periods of family worship, as Billy's father did when he turned to the story of creation.

These unplanned moments of worship, however, when God seems to reach out his hand into our daily lives to touch us are not enough. They are like the wild fruit one finds growing along the roadsides and in the woods—delectable and sweet, and sometimes hidden and growing in profusion. They truly fill us with a sense of the gracious bounty of life. But we find that in order to be assured of daily sustenance, it is usually necessary to depend upon the cultivated fruit.

Planned periods of worship are like the cultivated varieties. We seek assurance through them for a fresh and constant supply of spiritual vitamins to nourish and sustain us.

Our methods of cultivation and our patterns of worship may vary from time to time, and from family to family. But our purposes in maintaining them grow out of the common needs which worship within the family group satisfies. These needs are an awareness of God, a sense of family unity, and a true concern for others.

The patterns used by most families for their worship periods fall roughly into three groups:

1. Many families pause before or after mealtime for their daily reading of the scripture, a brief meditation, and a prayer for guidance, closing with the table grace or the Lord's Prayer.

For guidance materials they turn to one of the several devotional quarterlies or books of daily devotions which are provided by church denominations and church councils. The *Upper Room, Today,* and *The Quiet Hour* are typical of the devotional quarterlies available. They are prepared for either individual or family use, and tend to be written from an adult point of view. Magazines like *The Christian Home, Hearthstone,* and *The Christian Herald* have daily devotions planned primarily for family groups where there are children. *Thoughts of God for Boys and Girls,* prepared and published quarterly by the Connecticut Council of Churches, is a children's quarterly written on the junior level and prepared especially for personal use. However, its stories and worship enrichment materials make it easily adaptable for a family with children. In addition to these regularly published materials, there are many books on personal worship for each age level. (See your religious book catalogue.)

2. Some families have found meaning in longer periods of worship once or twice a week, or when some experience within the family life summons them to give thanks or seek guidance. These periods are usually leisurely and carefully planned. They provide an opportunity for the family to do many creative and instructive things in their worship. Many suggestions for this type of worship will be found in the pages of this book.

3. Other families, particularly those where there are little children, have found the bedtime hour best adapted to their schedules. Using that reflective period of time, when the work and play of the day is done, for recollection and sharing, for singing and telling stories, and for praying gives a sense of direction and unity to living, and it sends little ones off to bed in a happy, healthful state of mind.

Whatever the pattern for worship, its value can be measured against the purposes which family worship should achieve:

finding God, understanding one another, and sensing brother-hood with all people.

Perhaps you have not found a satisfying form of family worship which blossoms in your home into a pervading aware-ness of God's presence and an appreciation for one another. Perhaps you are just now contemplating the methods that will best serve your particular needs. Here are some guideposts, proved by the experiences of other families, which may help you discover the road to a meaningful formal worship period.

1. Choose a time when all or most of the family are to-gether and are unhurried. Even the small child who is old enough to eat at the family table can find some meaning in the practice of family prayers. And a relaxed atmosphere is one of the requisites for any spiritual exercise. The pressures of the unimportant which clutter our days must be set aside, and the attention of all focused on enduring values.

This is the initial step into meaningful family worship, and it is one of the most difficult. But difficult as it is, it speaks to the family through the voice of discipline, and says: "This is important; as important as unhurried eating and relaxed sleeping are to our well-being."

The family that cannot find unhurried time needs to examine closely the schedules of its members, and see if they are allowing the requirements of making a living or pressures from the outside to rob them of abundant life. For life itself is always more important than the things which sustain it.

There may be periods in the experience of every family when all or most of the group cannot be together and in a relaxed mood. Do not allow those periods to eat up any more months or years of your life together than necessary. During such times seek other methods of worship that will lift up your basic family loyalties. You will find suggestions in the following chapters of this book.

2. Select guidance material that has meaning for all or most of the family group. Most of us need some guidance. A worship guide is like a road map that directs our course when we are traveling through unfamiliar territory. We might possibly be able to find our way without reference to the map; we might even discover some interesting byways and places of interest not on the map—but we could also get lost. Few of us have sufficient experience or wisdom in the area of spiritual growth to chart our own maps and choose the most rewarding paths.

When we turn to guidance material, we frequently pick up that which is most accessible—a list of daily readings from a newspaper or church magazine, a quarterly of meditations from the table at the rear of the church, a devotional book selected at random from the church library or loaned by a friend. Seldom do we pause to ask, "Where will this guide lead? Was it prepared for individual or for family use? Are its language and concepts understandable to the children and youth in my family as well as to the adults? Does the scripture it suggests have meaning for the children in the circle, or will it create the impression in their minds that the Bible is a difficult, obscure book with little relation to their daily life? Does the guide suggest ways in which each of us can live our religion as well as think and pray about it?

If your family worship period seems sterile, do not blame yourselves or the practice of formal worship itself until you have examined the materials you are using in the light of these questions. The trail you have chosen may be too steep for little feet. The path may be too obscure for the eager enthusiasm of your juniors. Always remember that it is easier for you, as parents, to pace your steps with the short steps of your little ones, than it is for the child to stretch short legs into your footsteps. Likewise, adults in the family circle can usually find more meaning in worship materials which have been selected for their value to children, than children can find in adult-centered materials.

Choose guidance materials for your family with the same care you use in selecting a healthful and palatable menu for the family table. You place food there that will nourish your active, growing children, as well as food that will please adult tastes.

3. Keep with regularity the worship period.

How often the gardening attempts of our children are useless because when the first green leaves unfold above the moist, black soil, little fingers pull at them to see "what makes them grow!" There is time for the questioning attitude and the critical examination of our methods, but there is also time for patient and regular care, when we trust in the quiet processes of growth, and wait for the flower and the fruit.

4. Let each member of the family share in leading as well as in participating in the worship period. Mutual helpfulness blossoms into mutual appreciation when the ten-year-old prepares and reads the scripture, and assigns to his older sister the prayer, and to his younger brother the choice of a hymn, or when the kindergartner comes to daddy or mother for help in planning her "worship."

When each member of the family takes his turn in leading the period of worship, the family will be more apt to select materials of worship which have meaning for the younger members. When the family worship becomes a shared experience, each person in the sympathetic and congenial atmosphere of the home receives the training of planning, leading, and participating in corporate worship.

5. Don't expect the family worship periods to satisfy all the spiritual needs of the family. After all, each of us is a person with characteristics, experiences, and needs different from every other person—even those in the intimate family circle. Important though family worship experiences are, they are not enough. Certainly they are not enough for parents who face in their separate relationships, in their lives together, and in the guidance of their family, a whole set of experiences far beyond the knowledge and grasp of the children in the home. Certainly they are not enough for the youth in our homes, who throw out as childish, religious concepts always phrased in the language of the eight-year-old. Nor are they enough for the little child, whose expanding world is full of quests for those things which youth and adults have already explored.

There must be other times when as individuals, or as parents, or as parent and child, we seek guidance for personal growth, so that each may grow "in wisdom and in stature, and in favor with God and man."

So set the best time possible, select thoughtfully the guidance materials, keep with regularity the family worship period, and trust that the seeds are taking root, even though you may not at once be able to see the tender shoots spread into the soil of your family life.

Grace Before Meat

"WHAT ABOUT SAYING GRACE BEFORE EATING?" asked an earnest young mother of the child welfare speaker. "Isn't it just a superstitious hang-over that we should ignore? I certainly don't want my child to think she has to mumble something meaningless before she can enjoy the good food I've prepared for her."

Mrs. Brown rose from her seat before the speaker could answer. "We faced the same question a year ago in our home," she said. "Sally came home from nursery school one day, and asked, 'Mummy, why don't we say thank you?' 'Why, we do,' I answered. 'We say thank you many times every day.' 'No, we don't,' she said, 'not like they do at Tommy's house, and not like we do at school.' Then I realized what she meant.

"Neither my husband nor I had ever been accustomed to using a table blessing in our homes before we were married. We'd never even seriously thought about it. I almost resented her question. I didn't know how to answer her. Finally I asked, 'When we eat our lunch today would you like to say the prayer you use at school?'

"We bowed our heads at noon, and she said her simple prayer. That moment of quiet before we began eating did something to me. I realized we had been missing something. We have not missed it since. It's not that God needs our words.

But we need the grateful and gracious hearts that recognizing God has helped to give us."

The experience of the Browns is re-enacted daily in many homes. And many young parents who were skeptical of their need are led by an eager child to a simple recognition of the Giver of all good. Moreover, families who have learned to feel and to express naturally their gratitude to God find it easier to show appreciation toward each other. Saying "Thank you, God, for all your gifts," seems to make it easier to say, "Thank you, Sharon, for setting the table so beautifully"; and "Thank you, Mother, for making my favorite dessert."

Religion is that spiritual force which binds us together, and the act of grace before meat is truly an expression of religion. It is love for God and our fellow man set in the form of simple ritual. And like other rituals, it loses its meaning and becomes an empty form when the element of love toward God and fellow-man is absent.

One evening the father of a family who were accustomed to using the table blessing began filling his plate with food and picked up his fork without pausing for the prayer. The mother looked at him with surprise and young Billy asked, "Dad, didn't you forget something? Aren't we going to pray?"

"Yes, I did omit something important," the father replied. "But I didn't think this family seemed very thankful tonight. Billy said as he came to the table, 'Aw, Mom, why didn't you mash the potatoes?' And Carol said, 'Do we always have to have cole slaw?' Even little Terry said, 'There's that old spinach again.' Why should we tell God we are thankful for the food Mother has prepared for us, when our conversation is full of complaints? God does not want empty words. But if we are truly thankful, let's bow our heads and say our blessing."

If the table blessing has become routine in your home, ask yourself these questions:

1. Is our table prayer phrased in simple language that will have some meaning to every person at the table? There is real meaning for the little child in the simple gesture of folding his hands and shutting his eyes and being quiet for a moment. And by the time he is old enough to discover that words have meanings, he will listen for meaning in the table grace, or he will dismiss it from his mind as something that isn't intended to be understood.

2. Does your table blessing recognize your gratitude to God and express your willingness and responsibility to share? Is your family circle limited to "us four and no more?" True gratitude takes the world into loving consideration. An occasional meal when we deny ourselves our full fare in order that the hungry might be fed, a guest night when the warmth of our fellowship is shared with someone hungry for friendliness, or a frequent reminder in our prayers that all do not enjoy the bounty we know, are experiences that bring God nearer because some of his other children are also present.

3. Is the table blessing an experience which the whole family shares? Or is it always Father's responsibility? Or is it said only to please Mother? Or is the littlest child always expected to lead the family in the blessing?

"We used a table grace in our home," one mother remarked, "until Junior became self-conscious about the one he learned in kindergarten."

In some homes where grace is not used, the basic problem is a feeling of embarassment, or awkwardness in beginning, not an unwillingness to recognize God. Some families have begun the practice of bowing before the meal for a moment of silent prayer. The family that uses a blessing regularly will also find value in an occasional moment of silent thanks.

If "saying grace" is an empty routine in your home, try varying your method. Some families vary the form of their prayers from one meal to another. For example, in one home the day begins with a lovely morning prayer song, which the family sings to the tune of "Sun of My Soul":

> Father, we thank Thee for the night,
> And for the pleasant morning light,
> For rest and food, and loving care,
> And all that makes the world so fair.[1]

At noon the family repeats together a well-loved verse:

> We thank Thee, Lord, for happy hearts,
> For rain and sunny weather,
> We thank Thee, Lord, for this our food,
> And that we are together.[2]

Or perhaps in the midst of an active day the family sings:

> Love be with us at our table,
> May the food upon our board,
> Strengthen us and make us able,
> To do work for Thee, O Lord.[3]

And at the dinner hour the family clasps hands around the table and each in turn, beginning with the youngest, prays his prayer.

Occasionally when one family eats in public places, it bows for silent prayer before eating its food. Or if a member of

---

[1] Used by permission of Oliver Ditson Company.

[2] Odell, *Our Family Grows Toward God*, p. 25. (Abingdon-Cokesbury Press.)

[3] Brown, *Little Book of Singing Graces*. (Abingdon-Cokesbury Press.)

the family is late in coming to the table, he pauses for a moment with bowed head before eating.

In some homes, members of the family take turns in leading in prayer. The prayers offered may be either original and spontaneous, or prepared. If a little child is asked to take his turn in spontaneous prayers, the older members of the family should try to enter sincerely into the child's experience, and not be surprised at the strange sort of blessings he thanks God for. Small children learn what to pray for, and how to phrase their prayers from the prayers they hear adults make. Frequently we can help a child most, not by encouraging him to make spontaneous prayers that he cannot fully understand, but by teaching him prayer verses within his own knowledge and experience—prayer verses that he can learn to use with reverence and meaning.

In some families young people and adults alike enjoy the dignity of scripture passages used as a table blessing or as a "call" to the table prayer. The book of Psalms is particularly rich in such resources.[4] Dignified and reverent table blessings can also be found in the prayer books and books of worship of the various denominations.[5]

In the front of the recipe file box in our home a small space is set aside for table graces. Scripture prayers, traditional graces, and many singing graces are there. Copies of each prayer are typed for the entire family on 3 x 5 filing cards, using a different color card for each prayer. The child who helps to set the dinner table has the happy privilege of selecting the evening

[4] See the Appendix for scripture prayers that have been adapted for use as table graces.

[5] In the Appendix there are several traditional table graces from the books of worship of the various denominations.

prayer. He takes the copies of the prayer from the box and puts them at each place.[6]

Occasionally we sing a hymn. "For the Beauty of the Earth" and "This Is My Father's World" are especially reserved for our outdoor picnics by the lakeshore at sunset. During the Thanksgiving season the old German hymn, "Now Thank We All Our God," has special meaning for us, for we remember the story of its author, Martin Rinkart, the devoted German pastor, who served his townspeople during the pestilence of 1637. To the hundreds of sick and dying he brought a strong and comforting faith, and from despairing circumstances he lifted his voice in gratitude. The hymn reminds us, not only of those who are sick and hungry now, but also of the blessings and mercies of God which are sufficient for the sorrowing and suffering now, just as they were in Martin Rinkart's day.

A few months ago the children grew dissatisfied with their old, familiar prayers and begged us to suggest new ones.

"Perhaps it is better for you to pray your own prayer and forget the verses," we sometimes suggested. Duane had long before stopped repeating his memorized verse, but his "Thank-You - for - Daddy - and - Mother - and - my - friend - David - and-everything-else-Amen" became even more meaningless than the often-repeated verses of the other children. We tried to compensate by making our own prayers as meaningful as we could. But we knew eventually we would have to find new prayers for them.

"Let's write our own prayers," we finally suggested. And they quickly replied, "Let's do it tonight." Several times during

[6] Favorite table prayers from our file will be found in the Appendix. Most of them we have written ourselves as we have thought together about our blessings. Then we have set them to the melodies of familiar hymn tunes so that we can sing them.

the day Mother received little reminders that "this is the night."

Daddy and Mother did the dishes that evening while each child went off by himself with paper and pencil and made a list, as long as he wished, of the thoughts he'd like to include in a "thank you" prayer. The lists were lengthy by the time the dishes were finished, especially as the spirit of mutual stimulation set in.

Gwen, the youngest, went with us to the study first. She is fond of the little singing grace she learned at vacation church school, so we asked her if she'd like to write a prayer song of her own. We chose a simple melody which she knows and sings well, "Come Gently, Tread Softly." And then we copied down her ideas as she suggested them to us: "Daddy, Mother, big sister, my brothers, my family, food." These came first, and on the paper we wrote:

> For Daddy and Mother, my family, and food,
> For sister, and brothers, and everything good.

Then we thought of the "Thank You," and added a little prayer, phrased partly by Mother and partly by Gwen:

> I thank Thee, dear Father, and ask Thee to stay
> Beside us and bless us each hour of the day.

When eight-year-old Denny came in, his list was long indeed —everything from cowboys to wood and fire, with the seasons, birds, songs, animals, and pets high on the list. Houses, schools, churches, stores, the sun, moon, stars, and snow were also there. And of course Denny would never forget birthday parties, Christmas, Halloween, and Valentine Day. We grouped the ideas that belonged together and then wrote:

> For fun and food and love and care,
> For animal friends, glad times of the year,
> For trees and stars, and the big out-of-doors,
> For churches, and schools, and houses, and stores,
> I thank Thee, loving Father.

Charlene had already edged into the study with her encyclopedia of blessings before Denny was through. Her list abounded in her own appreciations: the organ, her cello, and songs; trees, flowers, snow, the day and night, beautiful seasons; family, friends, Girl Scouts, the church, and the Bible.

"Do you want to include something in your prayer besides 'Thank You' thoughts," we asked her.

"I think it's really important to share our good things," she answered.

And so her completed prayer, with each of us thinking it through phrase by phrase, went like this:

> Dear Father, for Thy gifts of day,
>   Family, friends, and happy hours,
>   For beauties of the trees and flowers,
> For music that I sing and play,
> I thank Thee, and I humbly pray
> That I may share Thy love today. Amen.

Nine-year-old Duane was proud of his list—all seventy-nine items. And he had thought of such practical wonders as the telephone and telegraph, and of Christmas and of games to play. He had itemized blessings like tables and toothbrushes, minerals and harmonicas.

"What's most important, Duane?" one of us asked as we surveyed all the possibilities.

"Why, Mother and Daddy, the family and friends, and food,"

he began to enumerate. "I'd like to put everything in, but I guess I can't."

"Well, maybe we can put down some words that will remind you of all of them."

And so we wrote:

> Thank You, dear God, for all good things:
> For love, and home, and food . . .

"We ought to find something that rhymes with 'things,' " Duane suggested. But we surveyed his sheet in vain.

" 'Brings' rhymes," he said. We scribbled down "each day brings."

"For happy times that each day brings," he finished.

"Do you want to include any other prayer thoughts," we asked.

" 'Good' would go with food. 'Help me be kind and good,' " he finished.

Then we read together what we had written:

> Thank you, dear God, for all good things:
> For love, and home, and food,
> For happy times that each day brings,
> Help me be kind and good. Amen.

We typed the prayers on the filing cards, and for a precious quarter of an hour we enjoyed them together, each child sharing his very own prayer with the others. Finally the cards were slipped into the recipe file box with the promise that they would be on the breakfast table.

The use of our own prayers has had particular meaning for all of us because each prayer reflects in a real way the personality of the child who uses it. And, each time we use the prayers, we are reminded of the thoughtful period that went into their composition.

Often the practice of using meaningful table blessings will become a prelude to richer experiences of family worship. The prayer may be expanded with a brief passage of scripture, a hymn, or a short devotional thought, into a brief but meaningful period of family worship.

And certainly a table blessing sincerely and thoughtfully used will influence, in an imperceptible way, the talk about the table that succeeds it.

Talk Around the Table

Styles in home furnishings change with the passing seasons. The overstuffed mohair living room suite gives way to the plastic-covered sectional furniture of functional design. The new television set requires a shifting of every chair in the living room, and causes the family to look, with more than passing interest, at the advertisements for "television chairs." In a subtle way the change in the furnishings of our homes reflects the shifts in our interests, our ways of life, and our values.

And when the round table in the family dining room gave way to the drop-leaf Duncan Phyfe, or the chrome-plated, expandable tables for the dining alcove, the family lost a symbol of value. For the family around the table is a *symbol of our oneness.* Around the family board we come together in unity.

In the era when the family shared most of its daily experiences, the hours about the family table may not have been so important. But today, when the father leaves on the early morning train before the children are awake, and when engrossing activities in school and community consume nearly all the waking hours of other family members, the period about the family table is frequently the only time when we are together. How important, then, becomes our use of these moments!

Here at the family table we give expression to the values and loyalties that matter to us as a family. Here the attitudes of

42

individual members are expressed and refined and brought into harmony with the basic loyalties of the family. Here the specialized interests of family members are blended into a pattern, a "family feel."

And this is a religious process. For "religion appears at the point where all the specialized values of life—economic, social, intellectual, ethical, aesthetic—are fused into a total meaning and worth of life." [1]

The word "worship" comes from the old Anglo-Saxon word "weorthscipe," and literally means something that embodies or exhibits the state or quality of worth. It is the practice of seeing into the heart of things and finding their real value.

The talk about our tables is one of our chief methods of communicating to one another the meanings and values that we have experienced. The everyday words which we use are our most common symbols of meaning and experience.

Of course, much of the talk in the family circle is concerned with the mechanics of living. Much of it is trivial—yet it is in the trivial, in the give-and-take of the common day that attitudes are shaped, habits re-enforced and patterns of value established. "In the dew of little things," a modern prophet remarks, "the heart finds its morning and is refreshed." [2]

"In the dew of little things"—in the talk about our tables our children "catch" our real religion. They discover what our true values are.

"All Dad cares about is making money," said a student to a college counselor. "And he doesn't care too much how he does it either. Oh, I know Dad would be shocked to hear me say that. He'd probably like to have me think that what he cares most about is being chairman of the church board of trustees. But

---

[1] Bower, *Curriculum in Religious Education.*

[2] Kahlil Gibran, *The Prophet*, p. 67.

you should hear him talk when he sees a chance to make an extra dollar—even at the expense of someone else!"

"The most important thing in Mother's life is her reputation as an immaculate housekeeper," remarked a college girl. "Of course, she feels she's scrubbed and cooked all these years for the sake of her family. But my brother and I often ran off to questionable places of amusement with our friends because we knew we'd hear about it if our gang messed up the house."

The parents of these students have failed sadly in conveying to their children the enduring values which will undergird them for times of crisis and testing, and which will give the buoyancy of joy to the common path of the everyday. If all the talk our families hear is concerned with the caring for their physical needs, what does that make of the home but a depot for food and a dormitory for sleep?

Let's make sure, for the sake of the way of life we value most and for the sake of those dearest to us, that what we say when we are together and relaxed, and the tone in which we say it, reflects the real "us"—not the jaded housewife, nor the tired businessman, nor the irritable, confined children. And let us also remember that the meal that begins with a recognition of the graciousness of God, the source of all good, has a better chance to continue with an awareness of the basic loyalties which bind the family together.

The talk about our tables is as important for healthful living as the menu is for healthful eating. Parents who spend the dinner hour discussing their own interests and concerns, and leave the children out of the conversation, have fallen into a habit of table talk which destroys the unity of the family. Soon a chorus of competing voices sets in that destroys any semblance of understandable conversation.

"I guess you must care more about your work than you care

about us, Daddy," said one six-year-old during a lull in the shop talk between parents.

And the oldest son in another home surprised the other members of his family by hiding the microphone of the tape recorder in the dining room. A playback of the table conversation led to some self-examination on the part of both parents and children.

"Let's try to talk about the things that interest all of us after this," suggested the oldest child. And thereafter the table conversation was dedicated to items of interest to all in the family circle.

Sometimes it meant a little forethought on the mother's part to throw out a leading question, such as: "What was the happiest thing that happened to each of you today?" Or on the eve of the first soft snowfall, "What was the most beautiful thing you saw today?"

Occasionally it meant a few moments of old-fashioned finger play, like "Simon Says Thumbs Up," while the mother and the oldest child served the dessert. And soon it meant, in the moments of prepared worship which frequently followed the evening meal, a greater unity of spirit, as the togetherness established during the mealtime talk blended into a recognition of loyalty to God and a seeking together for his guidance in family life.

The family about the table is also a *symbol of family democracy*. The old adage, "Children should be seen and not heard," gave way along with Victorian dress and manners, to the recognition that the family is the basic unit of our democracy. In the conversation around the table each makes his own contribution.

The period of discussion about the table frequently provides a time when individual members can bring for clarification and definition the questions, problems, and issues they face.

"They make the craziest rules at our school," nine-year-old Jerry said hotly one evening.

"For instance?" his father asked.

"They say I can't cut across Bill's yard on my way to school. He's my best friend, and I don't see why I can't take the short cut across his yard if his folks don't care."

"Maybe you misunderstood the rule," suggested his mother.

"No, Jerry's right," put in his older sister, who served on the school safety patrol. "We're supposed to report anyone who cuts across other people's property going to or from school."

"Well, I'm not going to pay any attention to a silly old rule like that," Jerry said. "It's nobody's business but Bill's and mine if I want to go to school across his yard."

"Wait a minute, son," said his father. "Maybe there is a reason for that rule. Remember the paths the school children wore across the Corey's lawn last spring? Mr. Corey told me just yesterday how he had worked to keep his lawn beautiful. But not until the school made the rule about keeping on the sidewalks did he succeed in growing a lovely lawn. He said he appreciated the way the school pupils have respected his property this fall."

"I never thought of it that way," Jerry remarked. "Dad, that means the kid'll have to keep off our garden spot next spring, too."

Thus the values that Jerry had overlooked were clarified through the give-and-take of family discussion.

One dinner time the Benson children were excitedly telling about the magician who had performed for the junior high school assembly. Eight-year-old Dick made his contribution to the discussion by remarking, "Jesus used magic; didn't he?"

"Why do you think so?" his mother asked.

"Well, he couldn't just touch people and make them well, could he, if he didn't use magic?"

"There are a lot of things we don't understand, Dick," his mother answered slowly. "The Bible doesn't tell us nearly as much as we'd like to know about Jesus and his influence on people. It just seems to give us brief little pictures of Jesus at work among people. But we do know that he had powers that no other man has ever had."

"Like when he just looked at people and made them want to live better lives?" asked thirteen-year-old Nancy.

"Yes, when men saw his goodness they felt sorry about their wrong ways and wanted to be like him."

"There's something else we're learning about Jesus' miracles, too," her father suggested. "The more we learn about the human body and the human mind, the more we discover that right thinking and right habits keep bodies and minds healthy and strong. Jesus understood a long time ago that goodness and health are closely related. When he forgave a man's sins, he also helped him find a way out of his physical sickness."

"Do you mean if I lived as good a life as Jesus did, I could just say to a sick man, 'get well,' and he'd be well again?" asked Dick.

"I don't know about that, son," his father replied. "But this I do know: if you live a good life, and seek as earnestly as Jesus did to do what God wants you to do, you will have the power and strength to help other people in ways you could never help them if you live a selfish life."

Often we cannot answer directly and fully the questions which our children ask. How, then, should we deal with the perplexing queries that crop out in family discussions?

Dick's parents, in the answers they gave, provide us with

some guidance. Honest inquiries deserve sincere, honest answers. And what if we do not know the answer? Do not fear to say, "I don't understand that either," as Dick's mother did. Recognizing the question, even though we cannot answer it, makes us one with our children in seeking the answer. And when we admit our limitations of understanding, we also recognize the mysteries of life. We open a door where God may enter.

The questions of our children seldom require dogmatic answers. It is better to define the issue and lead them along the way of discovering their own answers, rather than to impose our answers, which may reflect prejudice, upon them.

Periods of family discussion also provide an opportunity for individual members to share situations they cannot cope with alone. Perhaps the father faces a reduction in salary which will demand some revision of the family budget. By sharing the problem together, the family can work out adjustments that will be mutually acceptable.

"I don't really need a new coat this fall," fourteen-year-old Mary Ellen may suggest.

"Why can't I stop in and inquire about that after-school job at the drug store?" Tom, the high-school senior may ask.

"We don't have to spend so much money on shows and candy," ten-year-old Jim may put in, and Mother may decide that a sizable saving could be effected by doing her own laundry instead of sending it out. What looks like an insurmountable worry to the father thus becomes a means of binding his family together as they work out the solution to a problem involving all of them.

The discussion about the table also provides a way of reaching unity on our differences. Group discipline replaces parental discipline. The parents in families where there are several children are frequently aware that the children are able to handle many of the little differences that arise among them far better than if parents imposed adult controls.

The little child needs the security of controls from the outside, he needs to know what the expected pattern of behavior is, and he quickly learns that he is happier if he fits into it. As self-controls are developed, outward disciplines can be relaxed. The whole family shares in this process of gradually releasing responsibilities and privileges to the younger members as they prove themselves capable of handling more freedom.

One of the pictures from our family album which we treasure is that of seven-year-old big brother teaching his little sister to roller skate. He is holding her in front of him, supporting her in her attempts to keep upright with a strong, big brotherly grasp. Gradually he relaxed his support, until his companionship and interest were all she needed to give her confidence. This procedure is re-enacted over and over again in family life. And in the give-and-take about the family table the children often interpret to one another, far better than the adults in the circle could, the attitudes and experiences that have value for the family.

Occasionally the parents will also find themselves the object of the group discipline process.

"Will you be home this afternoon when we get home from school?" asks the eleven-year-old of her mother at the lunch table. "Oh, Mother, why not? That's the third time this week! Don't you know we like to have you here when we get home?"

And Mother realizes with a start that the sense of security and love she gives the family with her presence is far more important than the community activities or the bridge club.

The brief periods around the table in many homes are times of family decision-making and planning. Each person present has a chance to voice his interests and concerns, and together the family can decide the course of action which will hold the most satisfaction or value for the group. Some families refer to this period of discussion and planning as "the family council." Other homes experience a perpetual family council in which the issues of family interest are discussed, possible courses of action are evaluated, and a group decision is reached. This is democracy in action. And a democratic society is dependent upon a living democracy in hundreds of thousands of homes.

When there are small children in the home, it is well to recognize that there will be some decisions affecting the family beyond their grasp—decisions the parents should make. We do not help our children, nor do we help the cause of family solidarity, by expecting judgments from children in matters beyond their comprehension. Instead we are putting unnecessary burdens upon their young shoulders, which may give them a sense of instability and cause them needless worry. Begin by discussing those family choices within their grasp: Shall we go for a picnic or a long drive? What responsibilities must each of us assume if we keep the stray kitten that has claimed our home? As the children grow older, the area in which the family council functions can be gradually increased.

The discussions of the family council are often close to worship. For when we weigh values, we either admit God or shut him out! The more far-reaching the decision, the more important it is for us to reach a mutual agreement about it if we wish to maintain family unity. And the more apt the family is to feel the need for seeking guidance beyond itself. The family that senses God's continuing companionship in the everyday finds it natural and rewarding to turn to him in prayer when times of decision come.

The family around the table is also *a symbol of family outreach*. Perhaps the family circle has been temporarily broken, with a son or daughter away in the armed services or in school. Can the family that has known the joys of unity and democracy about its table ever sit down without a poignant awareness of the missing member? Without a thought of prayer that crosses the miles to sustain and strengthen the absent one? Without the realization that those who are gone are also reminded of home and the enduring values that home represents at the meal-time hour? The greater the area of shared experiences and values during the years that the family was together, the greater will be the influence of the family's values upon present experience.

In table talk, ideas from the outside also enter. In one Christian home where there are junior and senior high-school boys and girls, the dinner conversation often centers around a discussion of social issues in the light of Christian teachings. For example, what should be the attitude regarding race segregation at the community swimming pool? Jim Miller, the crack fullback on the high-school football team, has been denied admittance to the swimming pool because of his race. What are the implications for the young people in the family as they earnestly try to live as Christians?

Or what about political corruption in high places? Perhaps there is little the family can do about politics in Washington, or even in the state capitol, except to use its Christian influence in community discussions, and to support honest men at the polls. But when it comes to squashing an upsurge of cheating in the local high school, the senior who serves on the student council clearly sees his responsibility. And he knows that he has the support of his family in the unpopular stand he may have to take. The father, realizing the concern of his family, may be encouraged to undertake civic responsibilities he had previously shunned.

Occasionally the tragedies and sorrows recorded in the newspapers provide an opportunity for parents to interpret suffering and tragedy to their children in the light of their own firm faith. In this way parents can help to prepare their children for crises that they may have to face. Why do floods wipe out the homes of so many people every year? Why do accidents happen? These are questions every eager junior will ask, and parents will answer them in ways that either will build faith or will destroy it.

In some homes world concerns enter the family circle in subtle ways. The Morgan family papered the walls of their dining room alcove with maps of the world. Many times as they sat down to eat they were conscious of their fellowship with friends around the world!

"It made the whole world seem like a big neighborhood," said the oldest son when he left for missionary service in Asia.

Sometimes when foods from afar are served in one home, the mother will place the globe on the table between glowing candles, in recognition of her family's interest and concern for all of God's children. When her children made a set of small flags of the countries participating in the United Nations, she arranged the tiny flagstaffs in a base of modeling clay and used them as a table centerpiece. Sometimes she placed on the table a bowl of fruit from the Holy Land—dates, figs, oranges, even a pomegranate—to stimulate the family's interest in the land where Jesus lived.

Since earliest times the breaking of bread together has been a cherished symbol of mutual trust and friendship. The guests who come to our family table often enrich us. We try to share with them the best that we have, and at the same time we attempt to see through their eyes. The more their experiences differ from ours, the more they can bring to us. Citizens from other countries, members of other races, persons from a different profession or business from those represented in the family group, those whose hobbies differ from ours, can push back our narrow horizons and reveal to us a world of persons like ourselves with whom we can be friends.

In turn we can give much. We need not discuss religion, or even participate in formal worship together, in order to experience religious values. For whenever right attitudes toward God and fellow man, and toward life's problems are strengthened and vitalized, one of the purposes of worship has been achieved.

Have you ever stood before a towering oak and marveled that such a great tree could be nourished by the rocky soil? Into the earth the mighty roots go, to hold the tree erect. But the tree grows by means of thousands of tiny rootlets that break through the hard soil and force paths through the rocks. In the tips of the white rootlets there is an enzyme that dissolves the mineral substances of the soil, making it possible for the tree to use them for food. Without the quiet action of hundreds of thousands of such roots the green tree could not be sustained.

In the life of the family there are also enzymes at work. They are the attitudes we express in the little things—the tone of voice, the conversation around the table, what we do for one another, or what we leave undone. From the tender rootlets of attitudes come formalized habits, clearly expressed convictions, and finally the towering tree of a living faith.

Thy Word Is Our Lamp

IS THE BIBLE A "CLOSED BOOK" IN YOUR HOME? If it is, you are throwing away one of the soundest insurance policies your family has against the mental, physical, and moral ills that plague modern society. You are neglecting a sure safeguard of your marriage, a solid foundation upon which to build your home.

If the Bible on the shelf could speak, it would say, "I will make a difference in your home. Take me and use me." For the Bible has made a difference to every society and every home that has opened it and utilized its truths.

In the days of the decadent, morally-debauched Roman empire, the scholar Jerome translated the scriptures from the classical Greek and the little-known Hebrew into the Latin of the common people. About the same time, Ulfilas, a traveling missionary to the Goths and other Germanic tribes, translated portions of the Bible into the languages of the northern tribes. Did it make any difference? When the Germanic hordes invaded the Roman empire and the tottering, evil regime fell, a partly Christianized conqueror joined hands with the small but flourishing Christian community in Rome.

During the long, dark centuries which followed, the treasures of preceeding ages, the best that man had discovered about life, were preserved for succeeding generations in the Book.

The end of the Dark Ages was heralded by a fresh outburst of Bible translations in the languages of the common people. Wycliffe did not wait for the convenience of the printing press, nor for the bans to be lifted against interpreting the Bible to the peasant masses, to translate the Bible into the vernacular of the English people. He sent his "poor priests" into the hovels of peasants to chant words of abundant life. Those words inspired the English peasants to become free men. Thomas Huxley, the English scientist, refers to it as "the Magna Charta of the poor and oppressed."

During the fifteenth century, wherever the printing press was utilized, its first products were pages of scripture printed in the common tongues of the people. By the end of the century translations had been made into German, French, Spanish, Italian, Bohemian, and English. Serfdom in Europe was doomed in the light of Bible teachings.

The right to read and interpret the Bible according to their own understanding brought many early settlers from their European homelands to America. And the fundamental concepts upon which our nation was founded find their source in the faith which the Bible proclaims.

The modern family, with all of its improved standard of living, its abundance of material things, and its worship of the scientific method, has not outgrown a need for the Bible.

How can we read the Bible with real enjoyment? Many people today turn to the Bible but fail to find help or enjoyment in it because they don't know what to expect when they read it.

In the first place, the Bible is not one book. It is *a library* of sixty-six books which required more than a thousand years to write. It is a library with more than a hundred authors, many of them unknown, and unaware that they were writing for the future. It is a library of history, law, biography, poetry, songs, proverbs, sermons, letters, and visionary writings.

How do you use a library? Do you start at the top shelf and read straight through every book? That's the way many persons try to read the Bible. And if they don't bog down in the genealogies of Genesis, they get lost in the wilderness of Hebrew ceremonial law in Leviticus. Does every book in a library have equal usefulness, or interest, or value?

How does one go about finding his way in the Bible? In a library the reader turns to the card catalogue and looks up title, author, or subject matter. But few Bibles have that sort of guidance immediately available to their users. Some have limited concordances and some have interpretative notes. But the table of contents lists only the names of the books, and provides a scant guide for the reader who does not have a basic foundation of biblical facts.

A simple bookshelf diagram which children often make in church schools is an easy way to visualize the types of books in the Bible library and to anticipate what to expect when you open its pages.

When your child receives his first Bible, take time to help him find his way around in it. When you took him to the public library for the first time, you did not leave him at the door without the help of parent or librarian, and expect that he would find his way to his favorite picture books. Helping him get acquainted with his new Bible can be an interesting family activity.

If he opens his Bible in the middle he will open it at the book of Psalms. Help him find and mark the familiar landmarks in the songbook of the Bible. Although he still may be in the primary grades, he will recognize the twenty-third psalm as the Shepherd's Psalm; verses of Ps. 100 will be familiar to him, as

OLD TESTAMENT

MINOR PROPHETS	POETRY / MAJOR PROPHETS	LAW / HISTORY
Hosea	Job (POETRY)	Genesis (LAW)
Joel	Psalms	Exodus
Amos	Proverbs	Leviticus
Obadiah	Ecclesiastes	Numbers
Jonah	Song of Solomon	Deuteronomy
Micah		
Nahum		Joshua (HISTORY)
Habakkuk	Isaiah (MAJOR PROPHETS)	Judges
Zephaniah	Jeremiah	I Samuel
Haggai	Lamentations	II Samuel
Zechariah	Ezekiel	I Kings
Malachi	Daniel	II Kings
		I Chronicles
		II Chronicles
		Ezra
		Nehemiah
		Esther

NEW TESTAMENT

GENERAL EPISTLES / PROPHECY	PAULINE EPISTLES	BIOGRAPHY / HISTORY
Hebrews (GENERAL EPISTLES)	Romans (PAULINE EPISTLES)	Matthew (BIOGRAPHY)
James	I Corinthians	Mark
I Peter	II Corinthians	Luke
II Peter	Galatians	John
I John	Ephesians	
II John	Philippians	
III John	Colossians	Acts of the Apostles (HISTORY)
Jude	I Thessalonians	
	II Thessalonians	
	I Timothy	
	II Timothy	
Revelation (PROPHECY)	Titus	
	Philemon	

well as verses from some of the Thanksgiving psalms. Marking
the passages he already knows, and new ones as the family en-
joys them together, gives him a sense of friendly security in the
Bible.

Now have your child open the last half of his Bible in the
middle. He will find there the beginning of the New Testament. Here, too, he will see stories he recognizes. Help him find
and mark the story of the wise men finding the Christ child.
(Matt. 2:1-12). The story of the good Samaritan (Luke 10:25-
37), the lost sheep (Luke 15:1-4), the lost coin (Luke 15:8-10),
and Jesus blessing the children (Mark 10:13-17) are also familiar guideposts which will help him discover the Bible first
as a book of well-loved stories. There may be other familiar
stories he will want to mark. Take the time to find them. If the
family uses the Lord's Prayer, find it in Matt. 6:9-13, and pray
it together from your Bibles. Find the Golden Rule (Matt.
7:12) and the Beatitudes (Matt. 5:3-12). Take time as a family to enjoy some of these passages from the Bible.

In choosing Bibles for your children or a family Bible for
group reading, it is well to consider the advantages of a modern
speech translation. The familiar King James Version was translated nearly three hundred and fifty years ago, and its language
is the classic English of that time.

Since then, scholars have pushed back horizons of understanding about biblical languages and meanings. And important discoveries of ancient manuscripts have thrown new light
on confusing passages in the older translations. Several excellent translations have been made in this century by eminent
and dedicated scholars. The most recent version of the Bible,
The New Revised Standard Version, 1946-1952, represents the
combined efforts of America's leading biblical scholars. These
men have worked over a period of sixteen years to produce a

translation in modern English which still preserves the classic beauty of the King James Version.

An excellent activity for the family who really wants to do some meaningful exploring in the Bible is to build its own card catalogue. Use an ordinary 3 x 5 card file and enter your discoveries under subject matter headings—favorite stories, memory verses, character studies, guidance for specific needs and other appropriate headings. As you find a passage of value to the family, enter it by title, book, chapter, and verse in your file. If there are small children in your family, you will want to list several stories about the children of the Bible especially for them. As your juniors and youth study interesting passages in their church-school lessons, encourage them to enter their discoveries also.

Freely marking your Bibles, and writing in marginal notes as you explore them together, is another way to make your Bibles more useful for your specific interests and needs. It will also preserve your study for future use. The chart, "The Family Grows in Its Use of the Bible," in the Appendix, will help the members of your family find their way in the Bible on the levels of their own understanding.

In the second place, the Bible is *a digest* of religious experience. One does not glance at the brief synopsis on a book jacket and conclude that he knows everything within the book. Today when we turn to a favorite periodical or digest, we recognize that we are reading a condensed version and therefore must allow our imaginations to fill in the details.

The Bible is also a digest. Its pages cover more than two thousand years of human searching after God. The writing alone covers a period of about one thousand years. Many of its memorable and exciting stories have been preserved for succeeding generations by the loyal devotion of ancient storytellers and religious seers, who told their tales and chanted their wisdom around the ancient tribal campfires. As we read these ancient stories, it sometimes seems that much has been left out. Maybe it has! Perhaps the writer was setting down only a brief outline of familiar facts which he fully expected to be embellished and filled with life by a well-loved storyteller. Look what brief mention Methusaleh's 969 years gets! And who has not wondered what happened to the tower of Babel!

Even in reading the gospels one is aware that they are but a digest of the facts—only brief flashes of insight about the matchless life! The last of the gospels ends on the wistful note, "But there are also many other things which Jesus did; were every one of them to be written, I suppose that even the world itself could not contain the books that would be written." (John 21:25.) It takes imagination to read the Bible properly. There is such a great story to tell, yet only the outline is there! Our own imaginations and appreciations must supply the flesh and blood.

In the third place, the Bible is *a living book*. It is living in the sense that it is alive with action. There are weaklings in its pages, but the men whose names are written large—Abraham, Moses, David, Jeremiah, Jesus, Paul, to mention but a few— were men of dynamic action and winning power. They were tempted as we are—the Bible does not gloss any character or fault—but across the record their active strength shines forth, a challenge to all of us who take pride in accomplishment.

The Bible is living in the sense that its main story is continued. From its opening pages until its last, it is primarily a record of man's discovery of God, of his learning to live in right relationship with his Creator. That story is not finished. Nor will it be concluded in the current issue. Yet it gives meaning to our gropings to know what has gone on before, to see in a long perspective the mistakes of past nations, and to discover the enduring truths that still silhoutte man's skyline. In the words which Charles Rann Kennedy used to describe the living church, "It is yet building, and built upon."

The Bible is also living in the sense that its truths are rediscovered and relived by each succeeding generation. Each age, each family, and each person finds their spiritual searchings strangely affirmed and guided by the experience recorded in the Bible's pages. The Basque shepherd still lives the Shepherd's Psalm; the prodigal son still leaves his father's house; the sensible man still builds upon rock, the foolish man on sands; and all men still long for that day when "they shall beat their swords into plowshares and their spears into pruning hooks."

Therefore, because it is a living book, the reading of the Bible should not stop with Bible reading. Sometimes we will seek to apply its truths to our own daily living. Sometimes it will arouse queries in the minds of those in the family circle which will lead to a new understanding for all.

One excellent way to keep the Bible a living book is to find ways of high lighting its great poetic truths so they are near to us and available for our daily needs.[1]

Occasionally our children gain new meaning from its verses by "playing the stories." Searching for "the little lamb that got lost" or playing "Jesus' birthday" are spontaneous and natural expressions of the little child that give the Bible stories reality to him. Families where there are juniors may enjoy enacting some of the simpler parables of Jesus: the story of the talents (Matt. 18:23-35), the good Samaritan (Luke 10:25-37), the great feast (Luke 14:12-24).

[1] See the Appendix for *Worship Helps in Times of Need.*

Or perhaps you may like to vary the game of charades and play Bible charades by acting out one of its stories for part of the family to guess. (Other suggestions of ways to make Bible exploration a fascinating family activity can be found in Gebhard's *Enjoying the Bible at Home.*)

Bible reading brings both pleasure and understanding. One family has enjoyed over and over again some of the choice portions of biblical literature by arranging them for choric reading.[2] The family makes a small but almost ideal verse choir. High and low, heavy and light voices are there, and when the family reads in unison a fine sense of togetherness is felt. The family can study the reading to decide what phrases need emphasis and where pauses, crescendos, or sustained reading are suggested by the meaning of the verses. Then they can read and reread the scripture until a real sense of harmony is achieved.

Another way to keep the great spiritual insights available for our daily use is by memorizing scripture. There are singing verses in the psalms, there are profound moral depths in the prophets, there are gems of winning power in the teachings of Jesus, and there are notes of spiritual triumph in the epistles. All of these are truly ours only when they are "hid in the heart."

Many a good musician will confess that he cannot begin to "live" his music, filling it with the breath of his own spirit, until he knows it from memory. This is also true in the art of great living. The words that are hidden in our hearts have a greater chance to become truly a part of us. (The chart "The Family Grows in Its Use of the Bible" suggests memory passages on each age level.[3])

There is, however, one danger in encouraging children to

[2] See the Appendix for several scripture passages arranged for family choric reading.

[3] See the Appendix.

memorize scripture. How easy it is for children to learn verses that have no meaning for them!

One mother learned that the first-grade pupils of the public school her child attended were repeating the Lord's Prayer in a meaningless way. Consequently, she spent several afternoons with her child making a scrapbook of pictures to illustrate the prayer. As the two of them looked for pictures that would visualize each phrase of the prayer, they both gained insight into the true meaning of its words. This is an activity that has value for the entire family.

Because we frequently use, in family and in church worship, portions of scripture like the Lord's Prayer, the Shepherd's Psalm, the Beatitudes, and the Ten Commandments, we should find ways to fill them with meaning for our children. Talking them over—phrase by phrase with references to the children's experience—is probably the best way to make sure they are used intelligently. Another way is to use responsive interpretations occasionally in your family worship.[4] Perhaps after thoughtful discussion your family can work out its own responsive interpretations of some of the great passages of the Bible.

The Bible, of course, provides the family with its main source book for periods of formal worship. In order that its use may be a meaningful as possible, here are a few simple suggestions:

1. In planning your family worship, select a few verses that have unity of thought. Do not arbitrarily decide to read a chapter consecutively each day. Families who follow a prepared worship guide need to make sure that the scripture passages suggested in the guide have meaning for all the family.

[4] See the Appendix for responsive interpretations which our family has produced for its own use.

2. Prepare the reading. Particularly if one of the children is leading in he scripture reading, help him find it, mark it, and read it through ahead of time, so that he can read it to the family intelligently and without embarrassment.

3. Make sure that what is read is understood. If the passage has words in it beyond the vocabulary of the children, try to explain them. If the meanings are not within the children's comprehension but have value for their lives, take time to discuss them and apply the truths to their experience. You may want to use a modern speech translation or a children's bible story book. If the meaning of a passage seems obscure in the translation you are using, find it in another.

4. Try to understand the context and the background of the verses used. Who wrote them, and to whom were they written? For what purpose? Right answers to these question may change the meaning of the passage. For instance, the familiar Mizpah benediction, "The Lord watch between me and thee, when we are absent one from another" (Gen. 31:49), was spoken by Jacob to his brother, more as a threat than a prayer! A book like Goodspeed's *The Story of the Bible* will help immeasurably in giving you an understanding of the background of a particular book or passage.

If you follow these suggestions, you may find that you want other Bible tools to dig the riches from the Bible. There are several helpful tools available at most church and public libraries.

1. The Bible commentary. A commentary takes the Bible book by book, chapter by chapter, verse by verse, and explains its meaning. A good commentary will bring you the resources of modern discoveries and study about the Bible, which have greatly increased man's understanding of it. *The Abingdon*

Bible Commentary is authoritative and inclusive, yet it is written in language that the average layman can understand.

2. The Bible concordance. The concordance lists alphabetically the principal words in the Bible and the references in which each word occurs. One of our favorite family games is using the Bible concordance. One evening, for instance, we looked up the familiar rule, "Love one another," and found twelve references from the New Testament containing this command. The simple words took on a new meaning for us.

3. The Bible dictionary. This book, arranged alphabetically, explains Bible names, places, customs, and provides much other valuable information. *A Picture Dictionary of the Bible* by Ruth Tubby is simple enough for your primary child to use with enjoyment. Juniors, youth, and adults will find answers to their questions in the *Encyclopedia of Bible Life* by Madeline and J. Lane Miller.

4. The Bible atlas. Some of our Bibles have maps of the Holy Land, but frequently they are too small and sketchy to answer our questions. *The Westminster Bible Atlas* is an excellent source of maps of Bible lands as they were in Bible times.

5. The harmony of the gospels. Here is another Bible tool, which your family can create for themselves with a little guided effort. A harmony arranges the stories and teachings of Jesus from the four gospels in parallel columns, so that at a glance you can find, for instance, the birth stories as they are recorded in Matthew and Luke; the Sermon on the mount as it is recorded in Matthew and Luke; the calling of the disciples as it is recorded in all four gospels. A simple harmony can be constructed by securing from the American Bible Society two copies of each of the four gospels in the two-penny portions (price, two cents each!) . Get a loose-leaf scrapbook and divide the pages into four parallel columns. Then clip from your

gospel portions the references which you wish to include in your parallel life of Jesus.

It is an intensely interesting project, and it will open the life of Jesus to you in a way that no simpler exercise can. Children in the family will enjoy finding and mounting pictures to illustrate your family's story of the life of Christ.[5]

However, these Bible tools, or isolated Bible readings, or occasional use of the Bible at special times will never be a satisfactory substitute for sincere and regular reading of the Scripture in the family circle. Only by opening our hearts to its truths can it light our way.

[5] See the Appendix for references for building your own harmony of the Gospels.

The Hymnbook in the Home

THE BIBLE IS A LIVING RECORD OF MAN'S SEARCH for God. But that record stopped short nearly two thousand years ago. Today the hymnbook is the best contemporary recording of great religious experience which we have. It bridges the centuries from Bible times to this day, and lifts from the stream of life the poetic aspirations and the singing hopes that have sustained and strengthened the greatest and the humblest men.

When Charles Darwin, an English scientist of the nineteenth century, was nearing the end of his life he said regretfully that, if he had his life to live over, he would make it a rule to read regularly some poetry and to listen regularly to some music. "The loss of these tastes," he said, "is the loss of happiness, and may possibly be injurious to the intellect, and more probably the moral character, by enfeebling the emotional part of our nature." [1]

The family with a hymnbook upon its shelves possesses a digest of some of the world's greatest music. Leaf through the pages of a hymnal. There you will find themes from the greatest oratorios. "Joy to the World," which most children can sing, is a phrase from Handel's immortal "Messiah." "The Spacious Firmament on High" is a breath of lyric melody from Haydn's

---

[1] Kenneth L. Wilson, editor, "I Remember," *Christian Herald,* January, 1952.

"The Creation." "O Sacred Head Now Wounded" is an often repeated chorale from one of Bach's immortal oratorios, "The Passion of Saint Matthew." When we sing "Joyful, Joyful, We Adore Thee," we hear the "Hymn of Joy" which Beethoven used as a climax to his last and greatest symphony.

Glance through the index of composers of the hymnal's music. Many of the great are there—Bach, Haydn, Handel, Brahms, Mozart, Mendelssohn, Schumann, Sullivan, Bortniansky, Gounod—from the sixteenth-century chorales of Palestrina to the modern Sibelius. And on the page next to these are the folk melodies of the common people: Londonderry Air ("Above the Hills of Time the Cross Is Gleaming") , the Welsh melody "All Through the Night" ("God, That Madest Earth and Heaven") , traditional Hebrew melodies from the Yigdal ("The God of Abraham Praise") , the old English "Greensleeves" and "May Song" ("What Child Is This?" and "The Shepherds Had an Angel") , a Netherland folk song ("We Gather To- gether to Ask the Lord's Blessing") —and traditional melodies of Germany, Austria, France, Italy, Bohemia, Poland, and Greece. Early American folk music is there, too, and in some of the newer hymnbooks the best of the Negro spirituals have been included. You will also find the best in traditional church music, from the ancient plain song of the thirteenth century ("O Come, O Come, Immanuel") to the inspired phrases from the anthems of John Stainer and the modern melodies of Van Denman Thompson. The hymnbook on your piano or book- shelf is truly a treasury of melody.

Do the volumes of poetry on your library shelves—Milton, Tennyson, Whittier, Kipling—become dusty from lack of use? They do in our home. Yet we carry into every day the singing beauty of their greatest thoughts, set to music and bound into the hymnal.

Searching lines from Tennyson's "In Memoriam" are preserved for us in "Strong Son of God, Immortal Love." Samuel
Longfellow's evening hymn, with its chorus of "Jubilate's,"
"Now on Land and Sea Descending," and his fervent prayer,
"Holy Spirit, Truth Divine," are favorites for our family song
fests. John Milton seems less forbidding than he did in high-
school English classes when we sing:

> Let us with a gladsome mind
>> Praise the Lord, for he is kind,
> For his mercies shall endure,
>> Ever faithful, ever sure.

And Jonn Bunyan, who four hundred years ago, behind
prison bars, created the pilgrim Christian, of Pilgrim's Progress,
seems to speak to the youth of today when we sing:

> He who would valiant be
>> 'Gainst all disaster,
> Let him in constancy
>> Follow the Master.

> There's no discouragement
>> Shall make him once relent
> His first avowed intent
>> To be a pilgrim.

Bunyan is not by any means the oldest poet in the hymnbook.
The Bible had been canonized for only a short time, when hymn
writers began adding their religious insights to the spiritual
heritage of the race. Their poems of prayer are preserved in
your hymnbook. "Shepherd of Tender Youth," attributed to
Clement of Alexandria, was sung by the Christians of the
second and third centuries. Theodulph of Orleans wrote "All

Glory, Laud, and Honor" in the eighth century; and in the
twelfth century Bernard of Clairvaux composed "Jesus, the
Very Thought of Thee" and "Jesus, Thou Joy of Loving
Hearts." Beloved Francis of Assisi sang the "Canticle to the
Sun" ("All Creatures of Our God and King") in the thirteenth
century.

Modern poets and prophets also speak in the hymnal—Harry
Emerson Fosdick, John Haynes Holmes, Arthur Guiterman,
and John Masefield, to name but a few. And we can be certain
that the living religion of today, reflecting the imperatives and
the need for guidance in the atomic age, will be expressed in
the hymns that come from the printing presses this year and
the next. Our hymnal represents the growing edge of the religious heritage which we will pass on to the future. And the
hymnbook is open to your family, if it will only use it.

Some families have discovered that an occasional half hour
of singing favorite hymns gives the spiritual uplift that they
seek in family worship. But hymn singing is more enjoyable
if there are enough books to go around the family circle. The
hymnal, like the Bible, is not an expensive book. It often costs
less than a month's subscription to a daily newspaper, and for
the wealth of great music it holds, its value can scarcely be
equaled.

In one home where there were not enough hymnbooks for
the family group the mother encouraged her children to make
illustrated hymn posters as a rainy day and sickbed activity.
Looking for pictures to illustrate each phrase or verse of their
favorite songs, and mounting them neatly on a large sheet of tagboard, provided a much more fascinating and purposeful activity
than the dime-store coloring books or the paper dolls had in
the past. Church and church-school lesson folders, especially
those in color, nature magazines, and old Christmas cards were

ready sources for their pictures. The nine-year-old boy took over as his special task the printing of the hymn's words near the pictures, using his simple hand-printing set. Frequently the new hymn poster was displayed for several days on the worship center or on the family bulletin board before it was put aside to use during the occasional family song periods. To the younger children the hymn poster was easier to sing from than the hymnbook, and when the attention of all in the circle was focused on the poster a real feeling of family unity was achieved.

Of course, as the children grow older and want to sing the harmony parts they will prefer the hymnbook to the posters. They look forward eagerly to the day when they can be a family choir, the boys helping their father with the tenor and bass, and the beginning piano student taking mother's place at the piano.

But not all families are made up of embryo singers. In one family where the father shied away from notes of music on any page he delighted his children by playing all the family favorites on his harmonica.

A family with a miniature orchestra of string instruments discovered that the hymnbook was its most available and best source of simple music for the family ensemble. Playing together harmonious arrangements of Brahms's "Lullaby" ("Father, Send Thy Blessing"), Mendelssohn's "Consolation" ("Still, Still with Thee"), Haydn's "Introduction to the First Symphony" ("Come, My Soul, Thou Must Be Waking"), and Schumann's "Nachtstuck, Opus 23, No. 4" (Canonbury, "Lord, Speak to Me That I May Speak"), they learned the art of ensemble music through the use of immortal melodies.

But what of the family who have no musical spark in their natures? Are they to be denied the resources of the hymnal, just because some of them "can't carry a tune in a bushel basket"? The family record player, coupled with the wealth of excellent hymn recordings which are now available in both the inexpensive and the better-quality albums, is one answer. When our early-rising seven-year-old awakened the family with the strains from the record player, of "Holy, Holy, Holy" and "This Is My Father's World" we discovered a new and blessed use for the instrument. Mother frequently starts the hymn recordings spinning to urge the family to breakfast on time and in good spirits.

At the end of a long and difficult day we have found nothing better to relax the tense family than the quiet strains of well-loved hymns during the supper hour or just before bedtime. And after the day's excitement, when sleep is slow in coming to active youngsters, a persistent request "Play some hymns" will set "Day Is Dying in the West," "Softly Now the Light of Day," "Now the Day Is Over," and "O God, Our Help in Ages Past" to turning on the record player.

Some women have discovered too that hymn recordings lighten the drudgery of ironing or house cleaning more effectively than the radio soap operas.

Some families have found that the enjoyment of hymn recordings is a first step in establishing a pattern for family worship. Let's look in on the Brandon family.

"I won't interfere with your religion or your churchgoing," Joe Brandon told his wife. "Just don't expect me to go with you."

Lucille Brandon didn't. She'd like to have a blessing before meals, but except for lunch, when she and young Dickie were alone, she refrained from expressing the thoughts that filled her mind. Then one Christmas Joe and Lucille gave Dickie a small record player. Along with the nursery rhyme records they bought for the player Lucille got him some favorite Christmas carols and some of the children's hymns he liked to sing in Sunday school.[2] She even bought a few better-quality hymn recordings for her own enjoyment. Young Dickie soon seemed to tire of "Yankee Doodle" and "Three Blind Mice." But he played "Away in a Manger" and "Onward, Christian Soldiers" over and over again, singing the words lustily with the recording.

In the evenings after work Joe found himself relaxing in the big chair to the accompaniment of "Faith of Our Fathers" and "Blest Be the Tie That Binds." Occasionally he put down the paper and allowed the music to calm him. He discovered that he was listening with appreciative interest to the Bible stories Lucille was reading Dickie before he went to bed. And no father who loved his family could be impassive to the simple, trustful prayers a small child prays at bedtime. Joe's antagonism toward the outward forms of religion gradually melted, because the inner spirit had found meaningful expression in his own home.

"Lucille's doing a good job with our kid," he told his associates, and those who have seen the quiet but sure change in Joe admit that Lucille's doing a good job with her husband, too.

Another way the unmusical family can use the inspiration of the hymnal is to read together its great poetry. In times of perplexity or sorrow turn to Whittier's lines:

> I know not what the future hath
> Of marvel or surprise
> Assured alone that life and death,
> His mercy underlies.

[2] See "In Joyous Song," an album of religious songs for children, produced by Department of Children's Work, National Council of the Churches of Christ in the U.S.A.

Or on that day when one member of the family is challenged by new and unknown tasks turn to Maltbie Babcock's lines: "Be strong! We are not here to play, to dream, to drift."

The favorite periods for the song fests of some families may come at unexpected times—around the campfire after a family picnic, or at sunset when together the family watches the day silently fade away across a lake. Singing in the car on a family trip makes the miles fly by. We keep a half dozen pocket-sized songbooks, containing both fun songs and inspiring music, in the glove compartment of the car. And often the boredom of a long trip is lightened by rounds, folk music, Negro spirituals, and well-loved hymns.

A creative activity which some families enjoy is writing their own stanzas to favorite hymns. In a family where "This Is My Father's World" was a summertime favorite the oldest boy remarked, "It sure is too bad that the man who wrote that song left the winter out."

"Well, we don't have to," his mother remarked. "What are some of the winter joys that you'd like to put into the song?"

The family's list was long: snow on the spruce trees, frost patterns on the windowpane, warm clothes and hot food, snowbirds on the feeding tray, sledding and skating and making snowmen. Then the poets in the family went to work. Here are the lines they produced:

> This is my Father's world, and in the winter scene
>   The snow falls softly on lakes and woods
>   And sparkles on evergreen.
> This is my Father's world; I think of outdoor fun,
>   We like to sled and skate and ski
>   Until the day is done.

Their "autumn verse" for another favorite, "God, Who Touchest Earth with Beauty" reads:

> Like the scarlet of the maples
> Set my heart aglow,
> Like the sunset in the evening
> Let me Thy beauty show.[3]

Try it with your own family. Then put your verses on your illustrated hymn posters, or copy them on cards for your worship file.

Another family created its own scrapbook of stories of favorite hymns and hymn writers. When a book publisher saw their scrapbook, he asked for permission to publish it.[4]

Some families have found the stories of hymns and their writers invaluable resource material for family worship periods. *Lyric Religion* by H. Augustine Smith, which may also be available in your public or church library, is filled with worship materials adaptable for family enjoyment. Choice poetry correlated with hymn stanzas, biographical insights about the hymn writer arranged for oral reading with verses of the hymn, and the lining of favorite hymns with the scripture passages out of which they grew, are a few of the resources Dr. Smith has included in his book.

Another interesting way to use the hymnbook in family worship is to select one of the Bible-centered hymns like "All People That on Earth Do Dwell" (the Old Hundredth) and compare the Bible reference with the hymn that it inspired. Many of our earliest hymns were paraphrases of the Psalms or some other portion of scripture. In the days when every family could not have a Bible of its own, Bible truths were popularized

[3] For music see *New Hymnal for American Youth*, p. 223.
[4] See Bonsall's *Famous Hymns with Stories and Pictures*.

and interpreted by means of the songs which were used in worship. In the Appendix there is a list of some of the great hymns that are paraphrases or near paraphrases of scripture. Read the scripture passage, then sing the message.

"But the hymnbook is an adult book. How can I find resources there for my growing children?" a young mother asked.

The hymnbook, like the Bible, is an adult book. But one of the wonders of life is that some of the most profound truths are also the most simple. However, just as we choose carefully the stories from the Bible which we use with our little children, we must also wisely select the hymns that have value for the children in our homes.

Nearly all the hymnbooks of our churches have a group of hymns selected particularly for the children of the congregation, but there is a much wider body of the hymnody that can be used with profit and with inspiration for children.

Just as there are relatively few Bible stories that are meaningful to the preschool child, there are also relatively few hymns. But choruses, phrases, and brief responses from some of the hymns, like the response

> Come and worship, come and worship,
> Worship Christ, the newborn King.

from "Angels from the Realms of Glory," have value for even a small child.

How can you know whether or not a hymn is appropriate for use in the family? Here are a few simple guideposts to follow in selecting hymns for home use. Ask these questions about the hymn:

1. Is the hymn melody easy to follow? Is it within the voice range of the children?

The range of a little child is limited: probably from middle E to C. A primary child can sing easily songs written in a range from middle C to high D or E; and the average junior child has a range broad enough to sing most of the hymns in the hymnal.

2. Is the hymn a good length?

A small child's songs should be limited to a line or two; a primary child can sing a hymn of four lines; a junior can enjoy a full-length hymn. However, you may not want to use more than two or three stanzas of a hymn. Carefully select the stanzas that will have the most meaning for the children in the family circle. Frequently one stanza will make reference to death, or otherworldliness, or to adult sinfulness. Such references will only confuse a child.

3. Are the ideas in the hymn within the grasp of most of the family members?

Hymns which do not present clear mental pictures to children probably have little meaning for them. This is one reason for suggesting that children make illustrated hymn sheets of the hymns you sing together. A hymn which they enjoy illustrating will prove to be one with picture images and ideas within their grasp.

In selecting meaningful hymns, be careful to avoid those that are symbolic in thought and imagery. "The Church's One Foundation," for instance, is a great church hymn, but how many children will grasp the meaning of, "She is his new creation by water and the Word," or "From heaven he came and sought her to be his holy bride"? Children do not think in concepts or symbols; they think in images (pictures), and those images must be concrete facts within their own experiences.

4. Probably the most important question to ask is: Does the

hymn meet our family needs, express our aspirations, or give guidance to our present experience?

The usefulness of any formal material of worship—scripture, prayer, or hymn—is dependent on whether it takes us where we are and leads us toward God. At a time when the family circle has been broken by death, for instance, a hymn like "In Heavenly Love Abiding" or "There's a Wideness in God's Mercy" may provide a deeply satisfying spiritual experience. On the other hand, on a sunshiny morning when hearts are as glad as the day, "Let All the Earth in Every Corner Sing" or "My God, I Thank Thee Who Hast Made" may put into our day the lift that gratitude gives.[5]

But hymns, their music and poetry, are not the only resource which the hymnal provides for family worship. Church ritual is there, too, and while much of our church liturgy is beyond the grasp of children, some of the simpler worship aids and prayers have real value for the home. Use the same criteria in judging their usefulness that you use for selecting hymns: Is the worship sentence or prayer within the understanding of most of the family? Does it meet our needs, express our aspirations, or give guidance to our experience?

Find the prayers from the hymnal that have been prayed by Christians of all faiths for generations. Truly they express the universal longing toward God, and they are a part of the rich heritage which we should fill with meaning for our families and pass on to the future.

[5] See the Appendix for a listing of hymns that are meaningful for children and for youth, and are therefore useful to the family group.

CHAPTER
SEVEN

Worshiping Alone

IT STARTED IN THE VACATION CHURCH SCHOOL OF a village church and then spread into a dozen homes of the parish—a spiritual leaven which changed family life. When the junior class began its study of worship, the teacher found that few of her pupils came from homes where there were any religious practices—grace before meals in two or three of the homes, that was all.

"Can we make something in vacation church school that will remind us of God at home?" one eager little girl asked after the purpose of their study had been discussed. And so the class made altar triptychs—simple little stands of heavy tagboard—in which they mounted simulated stained-glass panels—by painting their designs in water color on heavy wrapping paper, inking the heavy lines, and then oiling the back of the paper to make it translucent. While they were working on their window designs, most of the children had slipped into the quiet sanctuary of the church and with patient effort had copied the symbols and designs from the beautiful windows for their panels.

Along with the altar triptychs the children took home booklets for personal worship, which were filled with their favorite songs, scripture references, poems, and prayers. They had often

79

enjoyed these materials in church school and were eager to share them with their families.

For the next several weeks, as the pastor called from home to home, he found the altar triptychs—in one home as a center-piece on the fireplace mantle with candlesticks on either side; in another, on a small table in the dining room, with the open Bible before it and the worship booklet near by. Some of the juniors had found a corner in their own rooms—a part of the dressing table, the top of the bookshelves, or a stand near their beds—where they had placed their altar triptych, with their open Bible, or a vase of flowers, or a book of prayers. It was a first step, in some homes a halting one, in recognizing and re-membering God. And some parents who had been indifferent and careless about religious values were urged by their children's interest to give thought to spiritual concerns.

Many Christian homes have found that a worship center is a helpful reminder of the goodness of God. One family uses the cabinet top in the dining room as a real beauty center for the home. There, beneath a favorite religious picture, the members place the lovely things that remind them of God's goodness: the narcissus bulbs pushing the first green spears toward the light, an oriole's nest found on an autumn trek through the woods, and between the bookends, a Bible, a book of prayers, and the family devotional guide.

A neighbor of ours has found another sort of worship center. When she moved into her new home, she was disappointed at first that the kitchen had no window above the sink.

"I'd have enjoyed the long vistas across the valley," she remarked. "I'd have liked to watch the children at play and the coming and going of the seasons."

But she set about to make the blank wall above the sink

beautiful. She hung there the fruit plaques that the children had made for her. And the butterfly picture her boy had mounted and framed one rainy afternoon.

For the empty space above the plaques—there where the window with trailing vines on either side of the frame might have been—she found another use. There she mounted a small white bulletin board, with a generous number of thumbtacks in the left-hand corner. A favorite poem which she decided to memorize, a prayer that voiced her own petition to God, the weekly devotional thought clipped from the church magazine —these soon filled the white board. Tacked onto the corner of the board was a cookie recipe simple enough for her ten-year-old daughter to follow, and the empty reminder pad her son had put there, "So you won't forget important things like peanut butter," he had said.

"They belong there, too, along with the devotional thoughts," our friend remarked, "just to remind me that my own God-given task is to be a good mother."

And so above the recipes and grocery lists, the dishes, sweeping and scrubbing, she senses a peace, an at-oneness with the true, the good, the beautiful.

Because group worship does not fill all our needs, the forming of meaningful habits of personal worship is important. Whether it is the bulletin board altar above the kitchen sink, the worship center in the dining room, or a junior boy's simple altar triptych and Bible on the corner of his dresser, the practice of personal worship gives poise and direction for daily needs. And the values gained by each member of the family in his own quiet time will be reflected and shared in the family group. Those values need not be discussed in order to influence in a real way the tenor of family life.

Teaching a little child to pray is one of the blessed privileges of parenthood. It is an experience which really starts before a child is born, for prayer is an attitude of spirit. It is an act of adoration in which the worshiper is filled with an awareness of God, his infinite goodness and beauty, and his Father-heart that desires most "to give what is good to those who ask him for it."

It is a spirit of gratitude that recognizes the blessings surrounding and sustaining life. It is an act of dedication to God's will rather than to self-will. And the indifferent, discontented, self-centered adult harbors attitudes just opposite those of prayer. Until we correct our own feelings of indifference, our spirit of dissatisfaction and malcontentment, our sense of self-sufficiency, and our habits of self-indulgence, we are scarcely ready to lead another to prayer.

When parents earnestly desire a full and satisfying life for their little ones and dedicate themselves—body, mind, and spirit —to make the good life possible for the life entrusted to their care, they take the first step in teaching their child to pray. And audible prayers with the child, if they express the sincere feelings of the parent, have value for both parent and child, even before the child can voice his own prayers in words.

Children learn to pray by listening to the prayers they hear adults make. They learn what is worthy to bring to the Source of all good, and they learn how to phrase their prayers. If the parent fails, the child may learn how to voice his prayers from someone else.

Fortunate indeed were the nursery tots in one church school which we knew. We often wished that every parent might watch the devoted Sunday-school teacher lead her three-and four-year-olds in their brief prayer period. After the children left their play and came together in a circle, they sang their "quiet song," a signal for bowed heads and quiet minds. And then the teacher led them. She prayed a simple thought: "Dear God, thank you for our play." The children repeated it after her. "We are happy when we are together. We are glad you are here, too. Amen." The parents of those children sometimes wondered at the natural, spontaneous prayers their tots prayed at bedtime.

An unhurried hour at the bedtime of our little children is sometimes a sacred necessity. This is the time when parent and child can gather together the tangled threads of the day's experience and sort them into a meaningful pattern. Then the little one can go to sleep with a happy sense of well-being.

Little Sharon cuddled close to her mother on the bed's edge. "It sure was fun playing with Tommy today," she said.

"I thought you said yesterday you weren't going to play with him any more."

"That was because he wouldn't let me play with his new wagon."

"And today was different?"

"We did what you said last night. We made up a new game that used my doll buggy, too." She reflected a moment. "Mummy, why is it more fun when we share our things?"

"That's one of the important rules for everybody to remember, Sharon. Even grownups are unhappy when they're selfish."

A few moments later when Sharon prayed her own prayer, she said, "Thank you for the happy day. Thank you for Tommy's red wagon and my doll buggy. Thank you that we shared."

Bedtime is a good hour for the spontaneous prayers of our children. And for our own prayers as well! For the parent who prays with his child as well as listening to his child pray is guiding him into a fuller experience of prayer. That parent says to his child, "You are not praying to me, but to God. I need God, too. Prayer is for both of us."

Moreover, there are many situations arising in family life

that can be best handled between parent and child in the reflective spirit of prayer. When a child has fears to overcome, or a decision to make when he faces a problem of social adjustment, either in the family group or in his wider relationships, or when he faces experiences of self-examination or penitence, he faces personal issues that usually require personal handling.

When you pray with your children, avoid theological language (including even the thee's and thou's) and symbolic concepts that have little meaning for a small child. Speak naturally—as a child to a loving father.

Does your child every hear you pray, "Dear God, I'm sorry for the quick words I spoke today; help me to be more patient tomorrow"? Does he hear you say: "I'll try to remember tomorrow, Father, to do the little things I had promised to do for the children today. Give me strength to satisfy their needs"?

How else is he to learn that God can forgive? How else will he know that you depend upon the Father to release you from feelings of guilt or indecision that fester and warp? How will he learn that God, with his infinite power, can give strength for both your needs and his? If he learns from your prayers that you trust in God's sufficiency, he will seek God for his own needs.

The parent who allows time for reflective moments with a little child can expect questions to come as the child seeks to define his relationship to the Unseen Spirit. "Who is God? Where is he? Can he hear what I say to him?" The parent's own experience of God and his faith in him must guide the answers. Strive to see through the child's eyes and phrase your answers in words meaningful to him. You may say, "God is like love—like the love of a father." Or you may say, "God is all goodness, and beauty, and truth."

However you answer your child's questions, remember that

he needs your affirmatives. He wants to be assured of your trust and faith in God. He is seeking a sense of security, of at-home-ness in his wider relationships.

Most of us know periods of doubt when our faith is tested. Even the Master, who was "tempted like as we," knew them. But when he prayed with his disciples and when he taught the multitudes, he spoke with certainty of his trust in his loving Father. When periods of doubt come, they are not the time to answer the questions of our young theologians. Let us face those struggles as Jesus faced them—alone in prayer. Then we will be prepared to meet the needs of young minds that are grasping for assurance in an expanding world.

There is another blessing that comes to parents who pray with their child. They learn to look at the world through his eyes of wonder. Our adult senses, sometimes dulled by the familiarity of the wonders about us, need exposure to the fresh vision of a child. We need to learn to see again. We need to learn to be thankful for the kitten's soft fur, for yellow dandelions in the lawn, for popsicles on a hot sumer day, for the robin nesting near the porch.

The time soon comes when the trustful kindergartner becomes the self-assertive junior and the independent youth. How can we help our older children find spiritual resources for their changing needs? How can we encourage them to keep their personal quiet times? How can we share with them the techniques for personal worship that have had value for us?

All the experiences of worship which we have had as a family group help, of course, to train for personal worship. By helping your juniors find and mark passages in the Bible that have special meaning for them, for instance, and encouraging them to memorize verses of scripture of enduring worth will give them familiar materials of worship which they will frequently use, perhaps unconsciously, for their own times of prayer.

Help them also to find devotional guides on their own level of understanding (*Thoughts of God for Boys and Girls* for your juniors, and *Power,* or some other worship guide, for youth). Make available to them books of prayers for boys and girls and for young people. Then help them think through their day's schedule to find a time for quietness.

One junior high school girl goes to her room as soon as she gets home from school. The house is quiet at that time. Her brothers and sisters are not home yet, and she has a few moments of reflective quiet for her own thoughts. She has arranged a simple worship center over the bookshelf in her room with a favorite picture above it. Occasionally she slips down to the piano bench after a few minutes alone and plays a medley of favorite hymns. "I'm just rounding out my quiet time," she remarked when her mother paused one day to listen.

Other juniors and youth have found that starting a poetry scrapbook of religious verse or a booklet of devotional thoughts or prayers that appeal to them, or even keeping a diary in which to record the best from each day's experience, provides a rewarding method of private worship.

Frequently they will seek to discover for themselves the techniques that have value for their parents. Ten-year-old Terry was an active lad. He often found it hard to go to sleep at night. One evening after he had tossed for a long time, he called to his mother.

"I just can't go to sleep," he said. "Mother, how do you go to sleep at night?"

"Some people count sheep, Terry. Others just lie quiet until they fall asleep."

"Mom, I mean how do you go to sleep?" he persisted.

"Well, son," his mother answered, realizing that his question gave her an opportunity to share a spiritual exercise which she had found helpful, "I try to think quiet thoughts. I close my eyes and try to relax every part of my body, and then I recall some of my favorite psalms—like 'The Lord is my shepherd, I shall not want'; 'I will lift up mine eyes unto the hills,' and, 'O Lord our Lord, how excellent is thy name in all the earth!' "

"And then?"

"Then I remember that I am surrounded by God's love and care, and I haven't anything to worry or fret about. I say, 'Into thy hands I commend my spirit.' "

"I'll have to learn more Bible verses if I'm going to use your way, Mother," Terry replied.

The parents in a family, who share a whole set of responsibilities and problems that often tax their wisdom, can also discover, in periods of worship together, resources sufficient for their needs.

After all, children are the product of two persons' love for each other. The basic understanding between husband and wife, strengthened and extended in periods of mutual seeking for God's way, is fundamental to the spiritual vitality of the family group.

Some couples have found that the Bible and devotional booklet on the bedside table will suggest a few moments of prayer together, either at the beginning or at the close of the day, when as growing adults their spiritual needs can have primacy.

"We used to quarrel a lot until we learned to pray aloud together," a young couple confided to their pastor. "And then we discovered we couldn't go to sleep with misunderstandings between us after we'd talked them over with God."

A wise mother once said to her grown daughter, "Remember,

you have a social responsibility to get enough sleep!" And just as each of us has a responsibility to those around us to practice the rules that insure physical and mental health, so we have a social responsibility to keep the laws of spiritual health. That means moments of quietness when we seek the poised and directed will that comes from being still and listening to God.

Harnessing Our Hobbies
for Worship

Your daily life is your temple and your religion.
Whenever you enter into it take with you your all.
Take the plough and the forge and the mallet
    and the lute,
The things you have fashioned in necessity
    or for delight.[1]

KAHLIL GIBRAN'S PROPHET VOICES THE EXPERI-
ence of families who have put loyalty to God at the center of
their life. They have made the happy discovery that the things
they "have fashioned in necessity or for delight" are all enriched because of their primary loyalty. And in turn their
daily work and their leisure-time enjoyments serve as channels
for expressing what matters most to them.

Among the lost words of Jesus are these:

Lift up the stone, and there thou shalt find Me;
Cleave the wood, lo there am I.[2]

Look about you, then, at the tools of your daily work, at the

[1] Kahlil Gibran, *The Prophet,* p. 88.
[2] *Oxyrhynchus Logia,* the Unwritten Sayings of Jesus.

instruments of your pleasure, for there is your temple and your religion.

Does a visitor in your home know by the physical surroundings which you have chosen to serve your family life that he is in a Christian home? Look at *the pictures you live with*. We cannot always select the views from our windows, but the pictures on our walls reflect in a subtle but certain way our values. And they wield an unconscious but profound influence upon the pliable lives of children growing up in the home.

"A picture is worth a thousand words," an old Chinese proverb says. A young woman who decided to devote her life to Christian teaching remarked, "It was the picture of 'Christ Blessing the Children' that hung on the wall at the foot of my bed that led me to want to be a teacher of little children."

Another youth was deeply influenced by Burnand's engraving "Go Preach," which hung above his desk. "Whenever I had an important choice to make," he said, "I could see myself in John's place in that picture, with the Master's hand upon my shoulder, and his other arm extended, pointing the way for me."

Fortunately, good prints of many of the great religious pictures are not expensive, and they are available through most of the denominational bookstores. One family found that the religious picture on their dining room wall became more meaningful to them when they changed it occasionally. They purchased a good frame and secured several favorite prints in a uniform size so that the picture could be changed before it grew so familiar that they looked at it without thinking of its beauty and meaning.

The modern paintings by the English artist Elsie Anna Wood, interpreting the life of Jesus, have a winsome appeal for children.[3] One family selected several of her prints and purchased three uniform frames: one for each of the children's rooms and one for the wall space above the family worship center. Occasionally they rotated the pictures. "On the Hilltop at Nazareth" became a great favorite of the ten-year-old boy, and five-year-old Sally liked "Of Such Is the Kingdom of Heaven," because "Jesus looks so happy. I like to pretend he's holding our baby," she added.

When you place a religious picture upon your walls, use it occasionally as the theme for a family worship period. Find the scripture reference which the artist portrayed in his painting. Select a hymn that the picture suggests. For instance, a family that enjoyed L'Hermitte's "Christ Among the Lowly" sometimes sang "Abide with Me" as they thought about the picture.

Study the details of the picture. Try to see the drama in the situation which the artist is portraying. Dr. Albert Bailey's *Gospel in Art* will unlock resources of many religious masterpieces for you.

After a family has enjoyed together some of the great masterpieces of Christian art, there will be times when the children will try to create their own Bible story pictures. The easel in the children's room may hold a kindergartner's attempt to tell the Christmas story or a fourth-grader's rough copy of Jesus blessing the children. Recognize and encourage their efforts to make graphic the stories you have enjoyed together.

Perhaps your family will find *other avenues of creative art* in which to express feelings of aspiration and gratitude. In one home where the family frequently spent evenings modeling in clay the mother fashioned her hands in the attitude of prayer.

"This is 'Petition,'" she said, placing the modeled hands to-

[3] See the Appendix for a worship service based on a picture study.

gether on the mantelpiece, "and this is 'Gratitude,' " she added
as she set her partially opened left hand model on the table in
the center of a bowl of fruit.

One wet spring day, when a rural minister was making his
first round of calls in isolated homes that had been snowbound
for several weeks, a farmer greeted him with the remark, "Say,
Preacher, I've got something for you, a bit o' whittlin' I did
when things were slow this winter."

He placed in his pastor's hands a set of candleholders with
delicately hand-carved arms, enameled until they shone in the
sunlight.

"They're nothing much," the man added, "but say, will you
put them on the altar at the church?"

Not everyone expresses his love for God in words of prayer
or songs of praise. Some may grow a garden full of flowers
in a spirit of wonder and gratitude, some may put the breath
of their own spirit into a lifeless lump of clay, and some may
"cleave the wood, and lo, there am I."

Turn to *your bookshelves*. How does your library serve the
values you count supreme? In addition to the Bible and the
hymnbook and other tools of the devotional life, let there be
books for the family story hours. Families who are old-fashioned
enough to snap off the radio and the television to read together
are blessed indeed.

One religious leader, reminiscing about his own parsonage
home, remarked, "I don't remember very much that was said
or done at our regular family prayer periods when I was a boy,
but the stories Mother used to read to us every Sunday afternoon stand out as though I were hearing them now."

In other homes perhaps it's a popcorn party in pajamas and
bathrobes at bedtime and a reading fest that will be long
remembered. Sometimes the reading progress may be slowed

by the stream of questions that halt the steady flow of the paragraphs. Answering your eager inquisitors is more important than reading the story. Be glad that the story opened the gate of their wonderings.

The stories you select need not be Bible stories; the books you read from need not be religious books to abound in spiritual values. Library shelves and publishers' lists have never before been so full of attractive and well-written Bible story books and fascinating tales of Bible times as they are today. Try reading to children *His Name Was Jesus* by Mary Alice Jones, or *The Bible Story for Boys and Girls* by Walter Russell Bowie, and see if they will let you stop at the end of the first chapter or the second.

When you select books for family reading, do not overlook biographies or short stories of great men. Find the stories about Albert Schweitzer, missionary doctor in Africa, about Sir Wilfred Grenfell, daring physician to the people of Labrador; about Marian Anderson, who sang first in a children's choir in her church, and about George Washington Carver, who prayed, "God, show me the secrets you have hidden in a peanut." Tell them about Mary McCleod Bethune, who discovered the true meaning of John 3:16, and about Toyohiko Kagawa, who helped to prepare his warring nation for peace.

Do not stop with the stories upon your bookshelves, or the bookshelves of your church and public libraries. Create your own. Take a newspaper sketch that tells of a gesture of unanticipated good will, or an article from a magazine that portrays integrity of character, and cast it into the language children understand. Make a story scrapbook or clipping file from your own casual reading that will be a seedbed for family storytelling. Give your children a heritage of greatness by which to measure their own growth. You may plant a seed in the mind of a future doctor, or scientist, or teacher, who now sits at your knee, which will bear fruit in the fullness of time.

Listen to *your radio*—with discretion, of course. Perhaps in your home, as in many others, you find your family seldom listens to the radio because there is so little of value that comes over the air. But there are some good programs. The family that begins its Sunday morning, for instance, by listening to a church program from the station of its choice, finds the Sabbath a greater blessing. The tired mother who dials to the afternoon hymn hour program at ironing time finds her spirits uplifted. The family that listens together to programs which dramatize stories from the Bible, then follows the broadcast with its own period of family worship, has discovered a resource that undergirds the values it cares about.

What of *your television set?* Christian parents sometimes have the distressing experience of hearing their tots chant the beer and cigarette commercials with as much vigor as they play cowboy. Children are as absorptive as blotting paper, and they absorb both black and white.

Stanley I. Stuber [4] sounds both a warning and a challenge to the Christian television audiences and the churches. He says:

There are enough Christians in this country to transform television into a mighty force for good. Television right now is glaringly pagan. It is in the hands of commercial exploiters. And they have no right to use this great means of mass communication against the public interest, contrary to the public welfare. It is right here that the church should put its foot down and insist that television contribute to the moral and spiritual well-being of the nation.[5]

[4] Chairman of the Public Relations Committees, Division of Home Missions and Joint Department of Stewardship, the National Council of the Churches of Christ in the U.S.A.

[5] Stuber, *Public Relations Manual for Churches*, p. 73.

But there are flickers of hope on the horizon. There are a few religious programs that are already proving the power of television to strengthen the moral and spiritual well-being of the nation. The good needs the earnest and loyal support of those who care what comes into their homes. And until there is much more that is desirable on television, the parents who care about the moral and spiritual training of their children will regulate the use of their television sets and will be wisely selective in what the family sees.

Perhaps *your record player* can serve you better than the radio as you lift up those values that you want to give primacy to in your home. Much of the great heritage of religious music —not only hymns, but the choral music of the masters, the organ and instrumental music of aspiration—is available on recordings. Even readings of choice scripture passages, with musical background, have been recorded by leading dramatic artists. Albums of "The Greatest Story Ever Told," prepared for radio dramatization of the Bible text, have been produced for home use.

And what of *the music you make* at home? That, too, can open doorways to worship.

A Christian mother with a gift of song began her morning with half an hour of what she called "vocalizing." And now as her grown children look back upon her daily practice, they do not remember the scales; they remember the arias of Bach and Handel and Mendelssohn which they learned to sing by heart from listening to her; they recall the story of the prodigal son, of the Pharisee and the publican, the singing verses of Psalms and prophetic chants of the prophets, set to glorious music.

"Mother gave us enough religion to begin each day by her morning vocalizing," remarked her daughter.

And the favorite lullabies for the foursome in our home are the strains of Bach and the melodies of Faure played on their mother's cello.

Your camera is another tool that can serve the values you feel are of worth.

Recently we projected some Kodachrome pictures we had taken of our neighbor's plain-looking house. But the pictures had been taken in autumn when the climbing ivy and the golden aspen in front of the house made splashes of color against the drab gray shingles.

"Who'd believe that beauty was at our front door!" he exclaimed. And then he added thoughtfully, "After seeing those pictures, our house will never look quite the same to me again."

When we lift up something that God has made beautiful and help others value its beauty, are we far from worship?

We stumbled upon another use for our file of Kodachrome slides. When we looked at the delicate alpine clematis blossom clinging to a rocky cliff, we could not help repeating, "Flower in the crannied wall . . ." And when we turned to the picture of spruce tips against the summer sky, we found ourselves saying, "When I consider thy heavens, the work of thy fingers . . ."

And so, with the family working together, we selected our choice pictures and our favorite nature scripture and poetry. Using one to interpret the other, we arranged worship services of our own that brought God near.

In the appendix there is a script that matches our pictures. If you ride the hobbyhorse of color photography, substitute your own pictures for our titles, and use your photography in family worship. You will look with new wonder at the things which God has created. Or select your own nature poetry or hymns [6] and illustrate them with your pictures.

[6] See the Appendix for a list of nature hymns to illustrate.

Better yet, come outdoors and bring the family. Let *your outdoor hobbies* put you on the pathway to God.

"I like dandelions when they're gold," said a seven-year-old, "but I like them better when they have white heads with a hundred wings."

Her father picked the dandelion gone to seed and asked her, "Do you know why the dandelion has wings?"

"I suppose so it can fly," she replied.

"To carry the seed away," her father answered, and he showed her the tiny seed at the opposite end of the "wings." "God planned it that way, I guess, so there would always be dandelions for little girls like you to pick."

The wonder of the dandelion seed opened the door into a whole realm of discoveries about seed dispersal which led the father and his children far afield, and often left them feeling,

> O Lord, how manifold are thy works!
> In wisdom thou hast made them all.

Another family paused with wonder akin to reverence when they discovered a chimney swift's nest in the fireplace of their summer home. There inside the chimney was the nest of twigs, glued tight against the sooty bricks by the swift's own saliva.

"Do you know any man-made glue that would hold a bundle of twigs like that against a sooty surface?" asked the father of the family. And when the family learned the habits of the chimney swift—how the fast-growing birds are forced out of the nests before they are strong enough to fly, but cling in an upright position to the chimney brick by digging their sharp tail feathers into the sooty wall—its wonder deepened.

"Daddy," said the ten-year-old, "things like that don't just happen, do they?"

"What do you think?" his father asked.

"I think God helped those birds grow that way."

The humble father of a boy who grew up to be a skilled scientist used to take his son by the hand at night and lead him out into the pasture. He would point up to the star-studded sky and say, "See, son, the heavens *do* declare the glory of God."

As his boy grew to manhood and his knowledge expanded, his views of the world changed radically from those his father had held. But he could not look into a star-filled sky without hearing his father's voice and sensing the wonder afresh that he had felt when his father had first said, "See, son, the heavens *do* declare God's glory."

Family Festivals

HAVE YOU EVER HELPED A LITTLE CHILD GET acquainted with the calendar? Do you recall how he marks off the year?

"Where's my birthday, Mother?" You find it; perhaps you circle the magic date.

"Where's Christmas?" You turn to December, and prepare next to find Easter, or Valentine Day, or your own birthday. From holiday to holy day he counts off the year.

Perhaps he is nearer to the truth, with his happy spirit of anticipation, than we adults. We forfeit much to the practical, workaday world. Let's not forfeit the glad anticipation of our holidays and holy days, for we need them.

Although we may not think of them as times of formal worship, they are really seasons of the spirit. Are they not the times we set aside the cares and concerns of making a living and keeping a house to enjoy life? Are they not the hours when we forget the things that sustain and regulate life—the clocks and schedules, the mealtimes and sleeping hours—for fullness of life itself? They are the times our faith in the goodness of life overflows into joy.

In this day of commercialism and exploitation how can we keep our festive times a natural, joyous expression of the bounty and goodness of life? It is easy to let the advertisements and misplaced emphasis of the commercial interests fool us and filch from us the real meaning of our festive occasions.

Here are a few guiding rules, if you would have the holidays serve your family as they should.

1. Develop your own family traditions for the day or the season. It may be a special breakfast menu that makes this day different from all others; it may be something you do together that gives this day an aura of its own. Perhaps you've a favorite story, like Dickens' "Christmas Carol," or special music, like Handel's "Messiah," that highlights the meaning of the day. Some family traditions will develop whether you plan them or not—perhaps too much turkey on Thanksgiving Day, or perhaps the football game via radio on New Year's afternoon. But you can select activities, too, which will give a special meaning to the season and which you do because they are a part of a valued family pattern.

2. Let the whole family share in the anticipation, the preparation, and the activities during the season. Your Cub Scouts may want to make table favors of their own boyish contriving. Your young adolescents may delight in trimming the home for the occasion. Your little ones may help make cutout cookies in the kitchen. Let the festival belong to all the family because all have a part in the work for it.

3. Share your festival with others, for joy has a way of spilling over. Do not try to keep it to yourselves alone. An occasional family celebration may belong only to yourselves, of course. But usually times of rejoicing mean opening the family circle to friends. And this is a time when the Christian family can look around them to seek out the ones who are alone, or those who have no children near with whom to share the day. Some families in university towns or near military camps have found

their holidays particularly blessed when they have opened their homes to the boy or girl away from home.

4. Highlight the festival with worship—some brief planned moments when you recognize that gladness and goodness are of God. "Joy is the thanks we say to God," an old song says, and we will find the day has a particular blessing if we remember the Unseen Guest.

Let's step around the calendar and pause at the holidays to see what values each can give to family life.

First there is Christmas. How can we keep a Christian Christmas? One almost feels at times that the season belongs to the shopkeepers and the money-changers rather than to the Christ Child, but we need not allow the tinsel of commerce to dim the holy star.

For Christmas is not a day—it is a season, a season of the spirit. If we would know its true values, we must separate the true from the trimmings, the gold from the glittering ornaments.

Analyze the familiar customs that weigh down the season to see if they have real values for your home. Then slough off the customs that burden rather than bless the season.

Begin your Christmas preparations early—your spiritual preparations particularly. Preparing to give is surely an exercise of the spirit. We try to put ourselves in another's place and, through the insight of love, select a worthy gift. Preparing gifts for others, planning special surprises for loved ones, earning a Christmas fund by their own efforts and then spending it according to their own insights, may open for your children experiences akin to worship.

Let even your earliest planning for Christmas be an act of worship. Some families remember those in prayer for whom they are preparing gifts. Other families plan a simple service of remembrance in mid-November, when they discuss together what they can do to make Christmas mean most to friends of the family.

The old and lovely custom of lighting the Advent candles is kept by some families. Each Sunday during Advent (the four Sundays preceding Christmas) a fresh candle is lit in a brief family ceremony. One family uses the Sunday evenings of December to invite other families and friends, whom it would like to know better, into its home for carol singing and popcorn around the open fireplace.

Some churches hold vesper services of music during the Advent season. Participating as a family group in the lovely services that churches plan for the Christmas season is another road to Christmas.

The symbols which you choose to place in your home at Christmas also can emphasize the true meaning of the season. The children in one home have made for the front picture window of their home a set of silhouettes that tell the Christmas story.

Ever since Francis of Assisi strove to make real the Christmas story to the peasants of the thirteenth century by arranging a life-size manger in the village square—even with live animals in it—the Christmas crèche has been a cherished reminder of the true meaning of Christmas. Your children will treasure the crèche that they make themselves for your home. The figures can be molded from papier-mâché or clay, carved from soap or cut from cardboard. Set them in a background of greens or on a tray, and place the crèche upon your worship center. One family found a lovely picture of the nativity and oiled the back of it so the picture was translucent. Then they framed it in a triptych folder and placed a light behind it for their Christmas setting.

Christmas is a time for song and story. The available resources—both in carols and in stories—are varied and rich. Your church can help you find the best for your own family.[1]

The climax of your Christmas preparation may be the family Christmas Eve service. Each year "Orders of Service for Family Use" are prepared and distributed by the churches.

We like to keep our service simple. We clear the table on Christmas Eve and leave just the tall taper burning in the birch log candleholder. By the light of Christmas tree lights and the single candle flame we sing our favorite Christmas carols. And then as each child shares some bit of Christmas verse or scripture which he has learned, he lights his individual candle from the center taper. Together we read the Christmas scripture and then join hands about the table in our Christmas prayers.[2] Each of us remembers someone else in prayer—a friend who is sorrowing, a loved one who is far away, a child in need. Sometimes we make a Christmas wish: that the angels' song of peace will come true, that the joy of Christmas will remain with us throughout the year, that all our friends may know a happy Christmas. We close by singing "Silent Night." Into Christmas Day we carry a blessed sense of peace.

New Year's Eve or New Year's Day is another time when a special service of family worship can lift up values a family might otherwise overlook. Perhaps your service will be simply a circle of sentence prayers seeking God's guidance in the new year. Perhaps it will be a discussion of your individual re-

[1] See Storms, *Roads to Christmas, Christmas in the Home,* Bethany Press, *Christmas Worship in the Home,* Methodist Board of Education, and others.

[2] See the Appendix for choric reading arrangement of Luke 2:8-20.

solves: what I want to do to make our home a happier place.[3]

Easter, like Christmas, is just a day on the calendar unless it is preceded by a period of spiritual preparation. There is a reason for the Lenten period. When the winter days lengthen and we begin to look for the first faint evidences of the growing season, it is well for us to think of the preparation of spiritual soils.

Lent is a good time to take stock of our Christian family habits. It provides us with an outward discipline to re-enforce our good intentions. It is a time for the family as a unit to resolve to attend and support the church and church school regularly, and to keep regular periods of family worship.

It is a time to remember the Master. Many churches make available to their families booklets of Lenten meditations. Whether you have a worship guide or not, use this period to relive the ministry of the Master. Select books like Walter Russell Bowie's *The Bible Story for Boys and Girls* or Mary Alice Jones's *His Name Was Jesus* to read to your juniors. Or read together *By an Unknown Disciple,* or one of the Gospels in a modern speech translation.

Jesus said, "If any man would come after me, let him deny himself and take up his cross and follow me." How often his followers have confused their little burdens of life with the Christian cross! The cross is an act of love, a symbol of sacrifice, which cannot be taken up except by means of self-denial. It is the second mile, the unexpected act of service, the unsought gift, the voluntary acceptance of responsibility, which we assume with willing hearts and hands, not for ourselves, but for our love of God. The family that finds an extra mile to walk in the service of others or who undertakes an added responsibility—

[3] See the Appendix for a formal family service.

perhaps in befriending a new family in the community, perhaps in making a gift for the relief of the world's distressed and needy, perhaps in assuming Christian leadership—will be preparing the road to an enriched experience of Easter.

In preparation for the day, Easter eve is a good time for a family service of worship. If you are a family of youths and adults, perhaps you will want to turn to the scripture account of the walk to Emmaus (Luke 24:13-35) and then enjoy together the familiar hymn, "Abide with Me," which was inspired by this experience. Or perhaps you will find inspiration in studying Burnand's picture of "Peter and John" [4]

If there are children in your family, place a flowering bulb upon the supper table, and read together or tell Henry van Dyke's story, "A Handful of Clay." [5]

Another holiday which the Christian family should make a holy day is Thanksgiving. Men and nations aware of God have always kept their periods of gratitude. We remember the early Pilgrim fathers on Thanksgiving Day; we should also remember their spiritual forebears and ours, who were singing three thousand years ago,

> O give thanks unto the Lord for he is good,
> For his mercy endureth forever,

and who built their calendars around their seasons of thankfulness.

Let your children make place cards for the Thanksgiving dinner table with verses of praise upon them. Perhaps a day or two before Thanksgiving your family could spend moments together to "count your blessings" and list them. Then using

[4] See Dr. Albert Bailey's *The Gospel in Art,* p. 393.
[5] See *The Blue Flower,* p. 201.

your list, write your own responsive prayer of thanksgiving to use for your Thanksgiving worship period.[6]

Hymns like "For the Beauty of the Earth" and "My God, I Thank Thee Who Hast Made" belong to a family Thanksgiving Day. The Thanksgiving dinner that begins with a glad hymn, the reading of the place card scripture verses, a moment of quiet to remember some blessing that brought special happiness, and then the praying of the family's responsive prayer will give a blessing to the family beyond full stomachs.[7]

And there are also special family times—your own private periods of rejoicing. Perhaps you celebrate on the eve of the summer vacation, or perhaps the first warm day of spring calls for a picnic in the park or near a lake with moments set aside to sing your joy and to give thanks for the green, growing earth.

If your home is like ours, the most anticipated days in the whole year are the birthdays of each child. Every family has its own happy customs of honoring the "birthday child" and making his birthday a special occasion. It is a day to speak especially our feelings of affection and appreciation for the honored one. In some homes he has the happy privilege of choosing the menu for the dinner, or of inviting his own guest, or of selecting a favorite activity for the family to join in. Perhaps your child selects the story for the extra-long story hour or chooses the dinnertime blessing.

In one home the children make gay place cards for the birthday dinner with Bible passages upon them. These "birthday blessings" are read around the circle before the father leads in a special prayer for the birthday child.[8]

[6] See the Appendix for typical verses.

[7] See the Appendix for the responsive Thanksgiving prayer prepared by a family with small children.

[8] See the Appendix for "Birthday Greetings from the Bible."

And at the bedtime hour is there a special birthday story to share with the little child? Small children love the stories of their own babyhood. When parents tell of the loving preparations that were made for the arrival of the baby, and when they recall the joys of the baby's first birthday, a child feels the assurance of the continuing love which surrounds him.

Let the adults in your home have birthdays, too! The birthdays of parents and grandparents are almost as important to children as their own. And those special occasions offer a happy opportunity to children to express their love and appreciation for the honored adult. Just as the little child needs our guidance in learning how to pray, he needs our examples and ideas in learning how to show appreciation to others. And he needs special chances to practice in order to learn the skill.

Another particular time of blessing for a family which can be highlighted by worship is that of moving into a new home. After the furniture has been arranged and the family has rested from the exertions of moving, plan a simple home dedication. You may want to share it with your neighbors and friends, or you may want to keep it for yourselves alone. Whether others are present or not, let it be a simple, sincere recognition that the living that goes on within the walls of your new home will be hallowed by God's presence.[9]

There is another festival day that can bless us if we use it rightly. It is the day which comes once in seven to give us respite from daily work, rest from routine and schedules, relaxation for body, and refreshment for the spirit. "Remember the sabbath day, to keep it holy," God commanded, and we would know more wholeness of body, mind, and spirit, if we kept his command.

---

[9] See the Appendix for "A Service of Home Dedication" or find the service in *The Book of Worship*.

Keep Sunday as a family festival. Make it a "festival of beauty, of loved things, of leisure, and of worship." Perhaps at your house it may mean a more leisurely, more lovely breakfast hour: a special coffeecake and an extra cup of coffee, a rosebud on the table, or a background of hymn music. Perhaps it may mean shiny faces and freshly polished shoes, Sunday-school offering jingling in pants pockets, the family together at church. Maybe in the afternoon there's time for family play, or a story hour, or a picnic, or outdoor games. At twilight after the supper dishes are cleared, maybe there is time for song, or for reflective talk by candlelight, or for marshmallows in the embers of the fire.

Let it be your special day to think a hundred times: "These things we treasure; this way we choose to walk; in the light of these values we live."

At Hallowed Times

THE THIRD, AND OFTEN OMITTED, STANZA FROM the much-loved hymn of joyous thanksgiving, "My God, I Thank Thee, Who Hast Made the Earth so Bright," reads:

> I thank Thee more that all our joy
>   Is touched with pain;
> That shadows fall on brightest hours;
>   That thorns remain;
> So that earth's bliss may be our guide
> And not our chain.[1]

Adelaide Proctor, the invalid poet who wrote this hymn of joy, knew something of the alchemy of sorrow and suffering. She knew that man's hallowed hours come not only in his times of rejoicing, but also at times when his human resources are wholly inadequate and he is thrown into the sustaining arms of God. When man faces tasks for which he feels insufficient, or when bitter disappointments shake his faith, or when he undergoes experiences of pain and suffering, or when he is faced by separation—either for a short time or by death—from his loved ones: these are tests that try his spirit and drive even the unbelieving to prayer.

[1] Quoted from *Best Loved Hymns and Prayers of the American People*, p. 30.

And through these experiences come the holy hours—the hours bought with broken spirits and contrite hearts. These are the hours when we are most apt to "be still, and know that I am God." And these are the hours when the man of faith and the family of faith reap the full reward of God-centered lives. For in their hour of need God is there to sustain and strengthen.

People with sick minds in overcrowded mental hospitals, and empty, jaded faces on the streets—these are tacit and tragic reminders of the price that millions are paying today for their lack of faith. The fact that they have no God to support them does not save them from trials and difficulties. In fact, it seems to increase the number of crises they face, and their pitiable weakness under the strain of trials is often their destruction.

Undoubtedly, the reason that so many families have failed to withstand the storms of our times is that they have left God out of their lives. They have no uniting loyalty greater than the selfish desires of the individual persons within the family. The times of testing reveal their divisions and strife.

All of us shrink from the testing that the crises of life force upon us. When Jesus taught us to pray, "Lead us not into temptation," he taught us a very human prayer. The Greek word translated "temptation" connotes any test, struggle, suffering, sorrow, or pain that comes—not necessarily a moral decision. And while we shrink from the experiences that try us, the tests that come with crises often reveal the true marks of character, and as often show weaknesses that need strengthening.

The family that depends upon God does not need to fear the time of trials, for God is there. The experiences we would shrink from, if we trusted in our own sufficiency, often bring hallowed hours that bind us more surely together as a family and deepen our confidence in the Supreme Value we have trusted. We read with new meaning, "Blessed are the poor in spirit . . . blessed are those who mourn . . . blessed are the meek."

The times of crisis—discouragements, dedication to difficult tasks, grief, pain, physical suffering, death—test the fabric of family life. How does crisis test the family? Perhaps if we better understand the nature of the trials a family faces, we can more trustingly put our hands into the hand of the Father.

In the first place the crises of life are a test of our love for one another. "Charity suffereth long," the scripture reads. Because of our love for one another the times of crises, even when they are personal, involve the family group. No one can see a family bow low in grief when tragedy or evil befalls one of its members, without realizing that one reason for the intensity of some family crises is our genuine love for one another. How often, for instance, a mother whose child is suffering would gladly take its place upon the bed of pain, if only she could!

A counselor who listens to the embittered and heartbreaking stories of family maladjustments realizes that one reason for the heartbreak is that love has been wounded. Except for that, the trivial slights would not matter.

How, then, does a Christian family meet this test of its love? By looking at its perplexities from the perspective of the values the family counts supreme—from God's viewpoint. When we feel ourselves in the great and understanding quiet of God, the tensions ease, and the confusing experiences that have disrupted life fall into their proper places, like the pieces of a jig-saw puzzle when one visualizes its total picture.

In the second place the time of crisis tests our growth. One of the purposes of family life is to encourage the continuing growth of each person. And so the little ones in the family are protected and nurtured by the older ones until they are able to care for themselves. The weak are supported until they become strong, and the aged are sustained until they receive their reward.

But let us not think that we are full grown when physical maturity or economic independence is reached. It is during the adult years that experiences of sorrow, discouragement, grief, separation, are most likely to come to goad us on to spiritual growth.

All life is a school, a preparation for that fuller life of the spirit, and those of mature years are most often subjected to the tests of greatest difficulty.

The writer to the Hebrews speaks of this truth when he says (12:5-7, 11):

> My son, do not think lightly of the Lord's discipline,
> Or give up when he corrects you.
> For it is those whom the Lord loves that he disciplines,
> And he chastises every son that he acknowledges . . .
> God is dealing with you as his sons. . . . Discipline is never pleasant at the time; it is painful; but to those who are trained by it, it afterward yields the peace of character. (Goodspeed.)

Wise parental love, like the love of God, may often involve giving children freedom to make their own choices—choices that may bring unhappiness and suffering if they make mistakes.

A thought like that must have come to the father of the prodigal son, when his younger boy came asking for his portion of the family wealth and for his freedom to do as he pleased. In the father's redeeming love, which first allowed the boy to go forth to learn the lessons he had not mastered at home and then welcomed the erring lad back when he had learned his lesson, we see the task of the home. The sustaining and continuing love of the family supports each member through the hours of his testing. And if the values which have had ascendancy in the family life are worthy, the hard-pressed sons or daughters will return.

Just as the remorseful son found his father anxious to forgive his misdeeds and all the suffering they had caused those dearest to him, so our homes too should ever be havens of forgiveness. For, after all, that is what "home" means.

Finally the hour of crisis tests our devotion. Our response to a crisis is ultimately more important than the crisis itself. For the way in which we handle our disappointments and griefs shows the fiber of our faith in God and in one another.

"I don't love God and Jesus any more," cried a rebellious child when the long-anticipated return of her father was delayed by a storm.

The little girl's mother was not shocked by her child's confused petulance. Instead she talked to the child sympathetically, trying to help her understand the circumstances and appreciate the greater values involved which her child's point of view had not seen.

There are also some adults who sound like the rebellious child.

"O God, why did this evil have to happen to me?" some cry. And then, like the Pharisee in Jesus' story, they proceed to tell God how good they are.

But the family that lives with a sense of God's presence and guidance does not know the rancor of such rebellion. It feels, rather, with the trusting poet John Greenleaf Whittier:

> I know not what the future hath
> Of marvel or surprise,
> Assured alone that life or death
> His mercy underlies.

"God's viewpoint is far longer than ours, daughter," a father once said to his grieving child. "Sometimes it is wiser to trust in his wisdom than to beat our heads against the stone walls of our own desires."

The family that is strengthened by a maturing faith will see in disappointment, as a poet has suggested, "His appointment." Some of the most rewarding roads we walk we would not have chosen alone. The finger of God, often in the form of a sharp disappointment or a tragic circumstance, points them out to us. From the perspective of months and years who has not looked back and said, "Thank God, I didn't get my way! Your choice, Father, was wiser!"

A family who faced an experience of disappointment was strengthened by the words of a friend, "Fortunately you are the kind of a family whose happiness does not depend upon what happens to you." The family that sees in its sorrows the hand of God leading it into paths of fuller service and deeper dedication knows the happiness that does not depend upon outward circumstances. That is the reward of a triumphant faith.

Moreover, as we face the tests of our devotion to God, we can be sustained by the truth that God in his infinite goodness can transform the experiences of pain, and even of evil, into blessings, if we only trust him.

A Christian leader of wide influence recalls:

The most sacred moment our family ever had together was the time after my father's funeral, when my mother gathered us children around her, and prayed that some blessing might come from my father's premature death. A short time later, my older brother gave up his plans to enter law school in order to prepare himself to continue the work our father had left undone. And I began then to make plans to enter full-time Christian service.

Christ takes up his cross, a symbol of cruel punishment and bitter hate, and makes of it a symbol of redeeming and sacrificial love.

When responsibilities come for which we feel ourselves wholly unworthy, we are led to say, "Not in my strength alone, O God, but with thy help will I do this task." The Church rituals of dedication—the baptism of a child, the church membership vows, the marriage ceremony—are formalized expressions of the inner need of each of us when we become aware of our own insufficiency and seek God's guidance to lead us through untrod and challenging experiences. They are expressions of our devotion to God and his way for our lives. And unless we see this purpose in the rituals of the church, the formal services, hold little blessing for us.

How can we prepare ourselves and our children for the shadowed hours? How can we make sure that we have the resources that will enable us to find God there?

All that we do as a family is a part of our preparation for the hour of trial. The techniques for prayer and the methods of worship which we learn to use effectively, the resources of worship—scripture, prayers, hymns, poetry—which become familiar and full of meaning for us through regular use, the values which we exalt in our daily living: all these gird us for the time of testing and steady us during the storms.

One family is using a simple technique to prepare themselves better for the hours of crises. In their card worship file they are recording the scripture references, the prayers, and the hymns that have particular relevance to experiences of testing which will surely come.

Have you ever sung a hymn and thought, "If only I could remember those words of assurance when my mind is clouded with fears"? Have you heard a minister read a passage of scripture and felt, "The next time I feel resentment or anger at someone, I'd like to recall those verses"?

In the appendix there is an outline of scripture references and hymns, selected for times of specific need. Place them in your file for future reference. Better yet, add to them the passages of strength and assurance your own study reveals to you.

When the hour of testing is upon you, here are a few rules of spiritual well-being to live by:

1. "Let every day be content with its own ills." Live one day at a time—or one hour, or one minute. Often what engulfs us is not the difficulty or weariness of today, but the dreaded anticipation of tomorrow. Do not borrow tomorrow's troubles. "Today, well lived, makes every tomorrow a vision of hope."

2. "As thy days, so shall thy strength be." (Deut. 33:25.) It is an old, old promise, made by a man of God to his people. And well might the once-hesitant Moses have urged his people on to new ventures with God! He knew the truth of this promise; he had lived it; he had found God's strength sufficient. The promise is just as true today. God gives us resources for the tasks he asks us to undertake. He gives us endurance for the sufferings we must bear. His strength is sufficient for our needs.

In the self-examination that comes with crisis we are often made aware of the weaknesses that need to be made strong. Pain, disappointment, and grief often make us teachable, by taking away our sins of pride and self-centeredness. Let us learn, then, to trust the lessons of adversity, that we may be made strong in God's strength.

3. If I do my part, God's forgiveness is infinite. And what is my part? To forgive the wrongs done to me, the Master tells us. To give up all feelings of resentment, all cherished grudges, all anger, all sense of having been wronged by another.

That is the only road to the cleanliness of spirit that makes it possible for God to relieve my distresses, to strengthen my weaknesses, and to heal my physical and spiritual ills. Medical science daily reveals that many of the diseases plaguing mankind are caused by spiritual unwholesomeness.

Before God can relieve my suffering, I must forgive, and I must seek forgiveness.

4. "Not my will, but thine, be done."

Our times of testing may drive some of us into the garden, where, resigned to a will we do not understand, we learn to pray, "Thy will be done." Then will come peace and strength.

The family determines to a considerable degree whether or not its members can learn to pray this prayer. For it is the climate of the family life which builds up a disposition to seek the will of God, even though at the time we may not clearly understand. It is in the home that we learn to trust his way, even when it leads "through the valley of the shadow." Our gardens of Gethsemane are on the way to the Cross, but they are also on the way to the spiritual triumph of the Easter morn.

Your Church Is Your Partner

On saturday evening sue reynolds and four-year-old Jimmy paused outside the church study. The light inside was on.

"Well, shall we go in?" she asked her little son. "Maybe the minister's here."

"I just stopped to ask what time Sunday school starts," she said when the minister came to the door. "Do you have a class for four-year-olds?"

The minister nodded. "And one for young parents, too," he said.

"You mean grownups go to Sunday school?" Sue Reynolds asked. "I always thought that Sunday school was for little children. Not that some of us adults couldn't use a little religion," she added hastily.

"Are you a newcomer to our community, Mrs. Reynolds?" asked the minister when she was seated near his desk.

"Just a visitor—indefinitely." She paused. "I'm staying with my husband's aunt for a while. Bill's overseas—a prisoner of war."

"I'm sorry. I hope our church can serve you while you're here."

"That's why I stopped in tonight. We're not church people, Bill and I. Both of us came from broken homes. Whatever religion either of us got, I'm afraid, was pretty superficial—just something to quarrel about. But it's going to be different for Jimmy."

"It's good to start him in Sunday school now, Mrs. Reynolds."

"I thought first of waiting till Bill got back, so we could talk it over. But when I saw the lights on in the church tonight, I felt I couldn't wait—even if he's pretty small, and even if we are strangers here." She paused. "It must seem strange to you, my coming here like this. But the weeks and months have been long since Bill left, and when I didn't hear from him for so long I felt nearly beside myself at times—about Jimmy. I wondered how I could ever give him the kind of training he ought to have, if I had to do it alone. And Pastor, I learned to pray. I've felt a lot better since I started to pray."

"I know," the minister replied. "I think we all do."

"The strange thing is, when Bill's first letter came through from the prisoner-of-war camp he said the same thing. He said, 'It's going to be different when I get home. We're going to pray together. We're going to find a church somewhere.' "

"I think the church has much for you, Mrs. Reynolds. When you come tomorrow, stop long enough in the beginners' room to get acquainted with Jimmy's teacher, Mrs. Russ. She's a young woman like you, whose husband is in the Air Corps. Then come up to the parents' class. They're studying a unit now on 'Fnding Help in the Bible for Our Needs.' I hope you'll stay for church, too. Somehow the hour in God's presence with others who are seeking him too can give us a sense of direction we may not find alone."

"Thank you, very much," Sue Reynolds said as she rose to go. "Jimmy and I will be here in he morning."

Sue and Bill Reynolds had found a partner in their task of parenthood.

The church is your partner, too. For your church is a fellow-ship of families like your own, bound together by their desire for the abundant life which Christ lived and taught. Your church has much to offer the Reynolds, your neighbors, and you.

In the first place *your church has tools.* The Bible and the hymnbook are its chief textbooks. Their resources for our spiritual needs are great, but most of us need help in finding them. One of the purposes of the Christian education program of every church—its Sunday church school, its weekday classes in religion, its youth activities, its study and fellowship organizations, its vacation church school, its summer camp programs, and its preaching ministry—is to interpret the spiritual heritage, found primarily in the Bible and hymnbook, for our present daily needs.

The church has found many ways to give its families tools for religious living. The church-school materials—the leaflets your children bring home from Sunday school, the booklets they study in church-school classes, the story papers they read on Sunday afternoons—are one set of tools which the church sends into the home. And they abound in resources for family worship, if parents will but use them.

Look, for instance, at the church-school leaflet your kinder-gartner carries home. Perhaps there is a religious masterpiece in color, or a picture story of children engaged in some friendly activity, or a picture on the front cover interpreting some Bible story in a way that has meaning for a child. It's a picture that can be enjoyed together at home. Then there's the story. The teacher has probably already told it at church school. But per-haps she hasn't. Perhaps she has suggested to your child that you and he enjoy it together at home. At any rate, the little child will want to hear it over and over again, until he can tell it to you, and perhaps to his toys. There's the brief memory verse: half a line long, but a nugget of truth simple enough for your child to grasp. On the back of the leaflet perhaps there's a note to parents—a few, well-phrased hints for ways in which you can help your child live the lesson through the week. Or perhaps there's a song, with music and all. The children will sing it on Sundays, and you can enjoy it with your family throughout the week.

The first songbook that one mother had for her child was a scrapbook in which she collected songs from the back of his church-school lesson folders. In less than a year she had a dozen well-loved songs in her collection, simple enough for her preschool child to sing. And when they washed dishes together, or straightened the house, or got ready for bed at night, she and her son sang, "When We Work and Play Together," "Friends of Jesus Must Be Kind," "Joy Is Abroad."

The primary, junior, and intermediate lesson booklets have many resources—stories, pictures, guidance in understanding passages of scripture, life problems for discussion—that can be used and re-used in family worship hours. Most of these materials are planned and written with the expectation that they will be used at home as well as at church school.

And there are the story papers. Recently we glanced through the literature book which our daughter in junior high school brought home for study. Fully a third of the short stories and poems that the seventh-grade English class was studying were reprints from church-school story papers. Not only are the stories in your youngsters' story papers interesting and well-written but they also lift up Christian virtues and attitudes.

Another set of tools which the church makes available to its families are materials specifically designed for home use: daily devotional guides, magazines of family enrichment, and in some denominations, booklets for the whole family related to the studies in the church school.[1]

Does your church have a library? Do you know what books are upon its shelves? A library of religious resources is one of the best tools that your church can provide for the families of its parish. Here you will find the basic tools for Bible study, the Bible in several translations, and books on hymns and religious art appreciation. In addition, books about guiding the religious growth of children, youth, and adults, books of games and handicrafts, and religious story books suitable for family reading can give a real lift to the Christian atmosphere of the homes in a parish.

There are other resources that the forward-looking church should consider making available to its families, too. At little expense the church could set up a picture loan library, from which families could borrow religious prints for their homes. The group-size teaching pictures used in the church school could form the nucleus for the collection. Gradually other prints could be purchased, mounted, and circulated.

With many families owning their own projection equipment and using slides and filmstrips for family entertainment, the church could well consider making some of the excellent slide and filmstrip religious aids available to its families on a loan or rental basis. The purchase price of a good religious filmstrip is about the same as that of a good book. A worship set, like "Let Us Give Thanks," or a set on Bible backgrounds, like "Adventure in Ourtown—The Story of Our Bible" [2] can open new vistas to the family that uses them.

[1] See booklets for home use like *Roads to Christmas* and *We Would See Jesus,* published by the Christian Education Press, and the home materials produced by the Presbyterian Church, U.S.A.

[2] Produced by National Council of Churches. See also the Audio-Visual Resource Guide (National Council of the Churches of Christ in the U.S.A.)

A record loan section of great religious music, scripture readings,[3] and dramatizations of Bible and missionary stories,[4] could also become a part of the church's library service to the families of the church.

These are all tools which have immeasureable value as resources for home religion, and they could be well shared cooperatively, for a single family does not put them to constant use.

But whether your church is large or small, rich or poor, look about you, and take the tools it is offering to you for Christian family life.

In the second place *your church has skills.*

When Sue Reynolds went to the parents' class, after leaving Jimmy with the teacher of the beginners, she found a dozen alert young people like herself, discussing the same sort of crises she and Bill had been going through. They did not assume that they had all the answers; but they were earnestly seeking guidance through the study of books, through the help of trained leaders, and through sharing their own experience.

"I had always thought that religion was concerned with some sort of other-worldliness," Sue remarked later; "but here I find out it's concerned with the tone of voice with which I speak to my boy, and with the kind of letters I write to my husband."

The church with a study class or a fellowship group of young adults, where parents can bring their problems, talk them through together, and find the best methods for solving them is building firmer foundations in the homes of its parish. Religion recognizes the whole of man—not just one little segment

[3] See *The Bible Speaks,* produced by The Methodist Church.

[4] *All Aboard for Adventure Series,* produced by Joint Religious Radio Commission and Protestant Radio Commission (National Council of the Churches of Christ in the U.S.A.)

of experience. Jesus came healing the sick, feeding the hungry, teaching the minds of men, and preaching a way of life. The church in its teaching ministry, while it does not try to answer all the questions of every parent, does help parents keep the values of life in their right relationship. It does point to skilled help in areas where it does not minister.

Another way in which the church gives us skills as parents is to ask us to teach in its church school. No teacher can teach unless he is willing and eager to learn.

When your church says, "Help us teach the children," think twice before you answer. In asking you to lead the church may be opening the door of better parenthood to you. The church-school teaching staff of most churches is an eager, teachable, stimulating group. The church, depending for the most part upon lay teachers, has had to select its best prospects and provide simple but challenging methods for training the unskilled. Think of the teaching staff of your own church. It is probably an earnest corps of parents whose primary concern is to keep growing themselves so that they will be able to lead others. Whatever leadership your church asks you to assume will reward you many times over by increasing your effectiveness as a person and as a parent.

Your church also offers your family the skill of its minister. Ministers vary in their abilities, training, and experience. But nearly every minister is in his profession because he loves people, and because he desires for them wholeness and abundance of life. Nearly every minister has had some training and experience in pastoral counseling. When tensions that make you feel the need of a friendly listener come into your home, seek out your minister. He will listen in confidence and in sympathy, and he may be able to point the way to help.

In the third place *your church has fellowship*. What Sue

Reynolds appreciated first about her new-found church relationship was its fellowship. When she stopped at the church study, she was a stranger—and she was desperately lonely. She left the church on Sunday morning feeling as though she had an anchor. She was surrounded with friendly faces, and she felt as though she belonged.

Jimmy Reynolds was as fortunate as his mother. He was as fortunate as every other little child who steps into the friendly atmosphere of the church nursery class for his first socialization experiences with other children. For there in a Christian atmosphere of sharing and mutual helpfulness, a tiny child, facing his first contacts in wider group life, feels secure and wanted. Truly, the most important teacher in the church school is the teacher of the youngest children's class. And the church's resource of fellowship means as much to the smallest child in the nursery class as it means to the oldest grandfather on the church roll.

Often the fellowship of the church becomes redemptive. Just as the sense of togetherness within a family unites the family —training and guiding the younger members, sustaining the old and handicapped ones, and upholding and strengthening the weaker ones—so the fellowship of the church provides a similar function for its families.

Jack Burton had a family any man would be proud of: an attractive wife and three eager healthy children, with the fourth on its way. Jack loved them dearly. But he had one weakness: he had a tendency toward alcoholism that periodically got the best of him.

Jack wasn't much of a church man. Carolyn, his wife, helped in the Sunday school, was active in the young woman's guild, and attended church occasionally. She sometimes asked Jack to go with her, and although he liked the church folk and counted the minister among his friends, he always had excuses of business or pleasure that kept him outside the church.

Alcohol began to get the best of him. He would be gone from the community a week or two at a time. His business was nearly on the rocks. Carolyn felt desperate. She considered breaking up their home. But she loved Jack, and she hoped that somehow he would come to himself.

Finally she sought the help of a few close friends within the church. A fellowship group of young parents determined that for the sake of Carolyn and the children they would do what they could to help Jack. The next time he disappeared a friend of his from the church followed him and brought him back while he was still in control of himself. They had a long talk together. His friend assured Jack that there was a circle of friends who would stand by him and who believed in his ability to overcome his weakness.

The families in the church fellowship group got together frequently for good times—without liquor. One of the men began dropping around to Jack's place of business each morning at coffee hour, just to help him ward off the temptation to have a glass of beer instead. Another stopped by the Burton house each Sunday morning and took Jack to church. It was not an easy fight. But because of the sustaining and strengthening fellowship of the church in which he is now a bulwark, Jack was able to make it.

Realizing the power of fellowship, more and more churches are building their programs with the emphasis on family participation. Sunday evening programs for the whole family, with fellowship hours before or after, monthly or bimonthly family fellowship suppers in the church, occasional church nights at home, family game nights at the church, have become accepted activities in the ongoing programs of many churches.

In the summer bulletin of a village church the following notice appeared: "Let's picnic together at the lake shore every Wednesday evening. Bring your food and dishes and family whenever the weather permits." One of the church members reported that the informal summer picnics had greatly strengthened the fellowship within the church.

The fellowship of the church also gives a family outlets for service. The church gives us handles of helpfulness by which we can express our concern for those in need. Let tragedy strike in a home of the community; how often the church is there organizing the good will of neighbors! Let suffering come to thousands on the other side of the world; the church is there, with our offerings, feeding the hungry, clothing the naked, sustaining the brokenhearted. Let us not forget that most of the great altruistic institutions of our day are children of the Christian church, and are maintained largely by church people.

The fellowship of the church gives your family and ours a chance to lift a little of the world's great burden of need and suffering. It unifies us as brothers of all mankind.

Finally, *your church has God.* All the tools, skills, and fellowship of the church have been one purpose, and that is to relate families to God. And the extent to which your church helps men and women, youth and little children, find God is the measure of the success of its resources, skills, and fellowship.

When a family begins to attend church regularly and together, something is happening in its life. That family has found in the church a partner. The roots of the Christian faith—recognition of God, discovery of the Bible as a spiritual resource, cultivation of prayer, and desire for Christian outreach—are sinking into the soil of that family's life. And with proper cultivation, the harvest of the fruits of the spirit is sure. And the altar of the church will become for that family a channel through which the forces of God can flow into its life, and through which its faith and loyalties can flow out to bless others.

There is an old story about a little chapel in the hill country of western Europe. It has no lights within. But as the villagers come at the vesper hour to worship there, each one brings his own candle into the church. Soon the darkened church is bright in the glow of many candles. And then by the lights they have brought the worshipers can see the inscription over the chancel arch: "I am the Light of the world."

Whether other families coming into your church find the church a partner in their responsibilities of Christian parenthood, whether they discover there the tools, the skills, the fellowship, and the living altar, will depend in a measure on the light your family brings to the church.

The Master has a word to the Christian family of today. He spoke it long ago to his disciples to make them sense their task as followers of his. He said: "You are the light of the world! Your light must burn in that way among men that they will see the good you do, and praise your Father in heaven" (Goodspeed) .

APPENDIX

Resources for Family Worship

Resources for Family Worship

TABLE BLESSINGS

Adapted From the Scriptures

O God, thou art [our] God, [we] seek thee,
.   .   .   .
for thou hast been [our] help,
  and in the shadow of thy wings
  [we] sing for joy.

—Ps. 63:1, 7

O Lord, how manifold are thy works!
  In wisdom hast thou made them all.

—Ps. 104:24

Praise the Lord!
O give thanks to the Lord, for he is good;
  for his steadfast love endures for ever!

—Ps. 106:1

Praise the Lord, all nations;
  Extol him, all peoples!
For great is his steadfast love toward us;
  and the faithfulness of the Lord endures for ever.
Praise the Lord!

—Ps. 117:1-2

It is good to give thanks to the Lord,
  to sing praises to thy name, O Most High;

131

> to declare thy steadfast love in the morning,
>   and thy faithfulness by night.
>
> —Ps. 92:1-2

> Our soul waits for the Lord;
>   he is our help and shield.
>
> .   .   .   .
>
> Let thy steadfast love, O Lord, be upon us,
>   even as we hope in thee.
>
> —Ps. 33:20, 22

Father: We give thanks to thee, O God;

Family: We give thanks; we call on thy name and recount thy wondrous
deeds.

—Ps. 75:1

Family: May God be gracious to us and bless us
   and make his face to shine upon us,

Father: That thy way may be known upon earth,
   thy saving power among all nations.

Family: Let the peoples praise thee, O God;
   let all the peoples praise thee!

—Ps. 67:1-3

TRADITIONAL TABLE GRACES

Bless, O Father, thy gifts to our use and us to thy service, for Christ's
sake. Amen.[1]

Give us grateful hearts, our Father, for all thy mercies, and make us
mindful of the needs of others; through Jesus Christ our Lord. Amen.[2]

[1] *The Book of Common Prayer.*
[2] *Ibid.*

O God, our Father, who giveth food for the body and truth for the mind; so enlighten and nourish us that we may grow wise and strong to do thy will. Amen.[3]

Our heavenly Father, we thank thee that
> Back of the loaf is the snowy flour,
> And back of the flour the mill,
> And back of the mill is the wheat and the shower
> And the sun and the Father's will. Amen.[4]

Transform this food into life, O God, and transform that life into useful service of thee; through Jesus Christ our Lord. Amen.[5]

> Be present at our table, Lord;
> Be here and everywhere adored.
> Thy mercies bless, and grant that we
> May feast in fellowship with thee. Amen.[6]

SINGING GRACES SET TO FAMILIAR HYMN TUNES

> Father, send Thy blessing,
> Gently as the dew;
> May Thy gracious presence,
> Keep us strong and true.[7]

> Lord Jesus, be our holy guest
> Our morning joy, our evening rest,
> And with our daily bread impart
> Thy love and peace to every heart.[8]

[3] *The Book of Worship for Church and Home.*
[4] *Ibid.*
[5] *Ibid.*
[6] *Ibid.*
[7] This may be sung to "Now the Day Is Over."
[8] Tune: "Canonbury."

Dear God, we thank Thee for this food,
  Through which we see Thy care,
Help us to grow more kind and good,
  Our blessings gladly share. Amen.[9]

For our family and our friends,
  For love and laughter that we share,
For good food that helps us grow,
  For Thy watchful, loving care:
Lord of all, to Thee we raise,
  This our song of grateful praise. Amen.[10]

For sun and shower, for soil and seeds,
  For love that fills our daily needs,
For hands that grow and cook our food,
  We thank Thee, Giver of all good. Amen.[11]

Lord Jesus, be our guest,
  Our food and family bless;
Help us each day to work and play,
  In love and thankfulness. Amen.[12]

This table is Thy table, Lord,
  Come dwell with us as we break bread,
And help us learn that as we share
  Thine other children, too, are fed. Amen.[13]

[9] Tune: "O God, Our Help in Ages Past."
[10] Tune: "For the Beauty of the Earth."
[11] Tune: "Canonbury."
[12] Tune: "Blest Be the Tie That Binds."
[13] Tune: "Lord, Speak to Me."

BEDTIME PRAYERS

Composed by Our Children for Their Bedtime Use

Gwendy's Prayer

Thank you, God, for your wonderful world,
  Thank you for warm clothing to wear;
For mothers and fathers, for teachers and school;
  Help us all to do our share. Amen.

Denny's Prayer

Dear God, I've had some fun today,
  And I've had work to do;
I've watched your little living things—
  They make me think of you
And how you care for everything;
  Please make me kind and true. Amen.

Duane's Prayer

For all good things I thank you, Lord,
  For food, for clothing, family, friends;
May I do my best at school,
  Your blessings on our family send;
Give through the night your loving care,
Be near to those who need my prayer. Amen.

Charlene's Prayer

Thank you, dear God, for blessings that surround us
  That are ours to share;
Help us to see the need that is around us,
  May we show thy care. Amen.

The Family Grows in Its Use of the Bible

Ages in Family	Level of Understanding	Portions of Bible Meaningful	Scripture to Memorize	Activities to Increase Bible Enjoyment
NURSERY 0-3 YEARS	Few, brief, one-incident Bible stories, often retold in short sentences. Conversation about pictures. First appreciates Jesus as a Man, Friend, strong, gentle, loving	Christmas story stressing mother love and care. Jesus and love of nature. His Father's care for flowers, birds, people. Conversation about Jesus and children		Looking at and talking about pictures
KINDERGARTEN 4-5 YEARS	Christlike action in play, work, service. Bible a book that tells about God and Jesus, source of loved stories. Stories, simple in structure (500 words) with rhythmic quality (repeated sentence or Bible verse as refrain). Likes to imitate storyteller	Elisha and home on roof. Gifts for the Tabernacle. The Baby Moses, Rebekah and the Stranger, Ruth and Naomi, David calling for Sheep. New Testament stories that show Jesus' friendly helpfulness, interest in people, love of God. Nativity stories	Only verses which child hears in relation to daily experiences, such as "Do that which is right and good," "Work with your own hands," "The earth is full of thy riches," "He hath made everything beautiful in its time."	Dramatize spontaneously familiar Bible stories. Free hand drawing on large sheets to illustrate stories. Looking at, handling, talking about pictures of favorite Bible stories
PRIMARY 6, 7, 8 YEARS	Reads simple family passages from Bible itself. Appreciates Bible as special Book: God's message of Himself and Jesus helps us know how to live. Likes to retell Bible stories and play them	Stories of Jesus' birth and boyhood, choosing his helpers, selected parables, helping others. Jesus' teachings about God's care, prayer, forgiveness, friendliness. Psalms and Scriptures of wonder and praise. Selected O. T. stories: Joseph, David, Finding lost scroll. Creation	Psalms 23; 100; 148; 122: 1; 48:9; 104:24. Deut. 6:4-6; Gen. 8:22. Prov. 20:11-12. Isa. 41:6. Matt. 7:12; 19:19; 22:37-39. Mark 11:9; 10:13-16. Luke 2:14; 2:52. John 15:14; 13:34. Acts 10:38; 20:35; I Cor. 3:9; I John 4:7; Eph. 4:32	Dramatic play, acting out stories in church school leaflets. Activities centered in childlife in Bible times—clay modeling village, dressing costume paper dolls. Bible games: Riddles, Charades. Unison readings, repeated responses
	Finds it full of meaning to have Bible of own. Ready for some knowledge	Life of Jesus from Mark enriched by other Gospels	Ten Commandments, Exod. 20. Beatitudes, Matt. 5:1-	Receiving and learning to use his own Bible. Choric readings

Age Group	Growth/Values	Content	Scripture References	Activities
JUNIORS 9, 10, 11 YEARS	of Bible background and history / Seeks for solutions of problems in Bible record of God's will for people / Better understanding of life and teachings of Jesus / Develops skill in handling Bible	Selected portions of O. T. history / Selected psalms / Life of Paul—stories of early church	12; 6:9-13; 28:19-20 / Luke 10:25; 4:18-19; 2:1-20 / John 15:11-14; 13:34-35; 3:16; 13:1-7 / Phil. 4:8 / Psalms 1; 24; 8; 67; 19; 117; 119:1-16 / Joshua 1:19	Family Scrapbook / Making Scripture greeting cards / Spatter painting / Dioramas, Bible character marionettes, character dolls / Nature Study: / Trips to museums and Bible exhibits / Bible games:
INTERMEDIATES 12, 13, 14 YEARS	Growing ability to find personal help in Bible and in ability to use / Greater understanding of Bible as record of a people seeking to know God, his outreach to people / Accepts Christ as personal Friend, Savior	Story of Hebrew people and their growth in understanding God / Psalms of praise and prayer / Matthew, Mark, Luke, selected portions of John / Selections of Acts, Paul's letters	Psalms 150; 104:14-23; 121; 46; 130 / Num. 6:24-26 / Luke 10:25-37 / John 15:1-12; 12:20-21; / I Corinthians 13 / I John 4:7-21	Choric readings / Exploring New Translations / Keeping Bible Festivals in the Family / Bible flower garden / Bible memory book / Visits to Jewish synagogue / Bible games
HIGH SCHOOL 15, 16, 17 YEARS	Grows in appreciation of way of life presented in the Bible / Sees in teachings of the prophets and Jesus values for social and personal problems of today / Appreciates relationship of Bible to other areas of learning; science, history, literature	Detailed review of O. T. message / Books of Esther, Ruth, Social Prophets, Job / Poetry of Bible: Most of Psalms / Prayers of the Bible / Sermon on the Mount, Parables and Teachings of Jesus / Paul's life and letters	The Sermon on the Mount, Matthew, chapters 5-7 / Romans 12 / Portions of Hebrews 11 / Selected verses from Prophets, such as: Amos 5:24; Hosea 12:6; Micah 6:8; Jeremiah 31:31-34; Ezekiel 36:26	Work out harmony of Gospels on life of Jesus and major teachings / Dramatic readings. / Put the parables, and teachings of prophets in modern speech, or in own words / Family Bible collection / Use of Concordance and other tools to enrich Bible study
ADULTS	Finds in Bible a source of power and inspiration for daily life. / Knows Scriptures well enough to use it sincerely and naturally to enrich family life / Finds satisfaction in interpreting Bible to children on level of their understanding	Uses those portions which have particular relevance to personal and family experiences / Studies to find values in parts of Bible unfamiliar or unmeaningful / Centers study in life and teachings of Jesus	John 14; 15; 16; 17 / Luke 12; 13; 15 / Great Teachings of Prophets / Selected portions from Epistles / I John 4 / Choose and memorize portions most potent for you and that fill your personal needs	Find ways to use Bible significantly in family worship / Plan family worship center with religious art displayed and changed from time to time / Tell Bible stories to children, reading a few significant verses from Bible itself / Guide activities of family

From *Enjoying the Bible at Home* (copyright). Used by permission the Christian Board of Publication.

FAMILY CHORIC READINGS

The Parable of the Builders

Matt. 7:24-28

To Be Read in Unison:

Every one then / who *hears* these words of mine / and *does* them / will be like a *wise* man / who built his house upon the rock; / (gradual crescendo) and the rain fell, and the floods came, and the winds blew and *beat* upon that house, / but it did *not fall,* because it had been *founded* on the *rock.* And every one who hears these words of mine and does *not* do them / will be like a *foolish* man / who built *his* house upon the *sand;* / and the rain fell, / and the floods came, / and the winds blew / and *beat against that house,* and it *fell;* / and *great* was the fall of *it.*

Ps. 121

Mother: (questingly)   I lift up my eyes to the hills.
                         From whence does my help come?

Father: (exaltingly)   My help comes from the Lord,
                         who made heaven and earth.

Children: He will not let your feet be moved,
                         he who keeps you will not slumber.

All: (with emphasis)   *Behold,* he who *keeps* Israel
                         will neither slumber nor sleep.

     (deliberately)   The *Lord* is *your* keeper;
                         the *Lord* is your shade
                         on your right hand.
                         The sun shall not smite you by day,
                         nor the moon by night.
                         The *Lord* will keep you from all evil;
                         he will keep your life.

     (sustained)   The Lord will keep
                         your going out and your coming in
                         from this time forth and for evermore.

Mother: I lift up my eyes to the hills.
                         From whence does my help come?

All: My help comes from the Lord,
                         who made heaven and earth.

The Christmas Story

Luke 2:8-20

Father: And in that region / there were *shepherds* out in the field, keeping watch over their *flock* by night.

Mother: And an *angel of the Lord* appeared to them, / and the *glory of the Lord* shone around them, / and they were filled with fear. / And the angel said to them,

First Child: Be not *afraid;* for behold, / I bring you good news of a great joy which will come to all the people; for to you is born this day in the city of David a *Savior,* / who is *Christ the Lord.* / And this will be a *sign* for you: / You will find a *babe* wrapped in swaddling cloths / and lying in a manger.

Boys: And *suddenly* / there was with the angel / a multitude of the heavenly host / *praising God* / and saying,

Girls: *Glory to God* in the highest, and on earth *peace* among men with whom he is pleased!

Boys: When the angels went away from them into heaven, the shepherds said to one another,

Father: Let us *go* over to Bethlehem / and *see* this thing that has happened, / which the Lord has made *known* to *us.*

All: (hurriedly) And they *went with haste,* and found *Mary* / and *Joseph,* / and the *babe* lying in a manger.

Father: And when they saw it / they made known the *saying* / which had been told them *concerning* this child;

Boys: And all who heard it wondered / at what the shepherds told them.

Mother: But *Mary* / kept all these things, / *pondering* them in her heart.

Father: And the shepherds *returned,* / *glorifying* and *praising God* for all they had *heard* and *seen,* / as it had been told them.

All: For *God* so *loved* the world / that he *gave* his only *Son,* that whoever believes in him / should *not* perish / but have *eternal life.* (John 3:16.)

THE LOVE CHAPTER

I Cor. 12:31; 13:1-8, 13

Father:	I will show you a still more excellent way.
First Child:	If I speak in the tongues of men and of angels, but have not love, I am a noisy gong or a clanging cymbal.
Second Child:	And if I have prophetic powers, and understand all mysteries and all knowledge, and if I have all faith, so as to remove mountains, but have not love, I am nothing.
Third Child:	If I give away all I have, and if I deliver my body to be burned, but have no love, I gain nothing.
All:	Love is patient and kind;
First Child:	Love is not jealous or boastful; it is not arrogant or rude.
Second Child:	Love does not insist on its own way; it is not irritable or resentful;
Third Child:	It does not rejoice at wrong, but rejoices in the right.
Mother:	Love bears all things, believes all things, hopes all things, endures all things.
All:	Love never ends.
Father:	So faith, hope, love abide, these three;
All:	But the greatest of these is love.

THE SHEPHERD'S PSALM

Ps. 23 (K.J.V.)

First Child:	The Lord is my shepherd; I shall not want.
Second Child:	David, the shepherd boy, who may have written this psalm, was only one of the many shepherds the Bible tells us about. He woke early each morning, just as the eastern sky was tinted with the rose of sunrise. Then he went to the sheepfold and called his sheep.
First Child:	He maketh me to lie down in green pastures.
Second Child:	During the dry season the land was scorched and brown, and the shepherd lad often had to lead his sheep far up into the hills where htye found green pasture.

First Child: He leadeth me beside the still waters.

Second Child: Mountain streams are often swift and deep. Where the current flows fast ,the timid sheep would be afraid to drink. So David looked for still pools where the sheep could drink safely, or he dammed up a bend in the stream so that the swift waters would not frighten the sheep.

First Child: He restoreth my soul: he leadeth me in the paths of righteousness for his name's sake.

Second Child: There were many choices the shepherd boy had to make. If a careless sheep damaged the neighbor's crops, the owner of the land could claim the sheep for damage. In the rainy season the sheep paths might be washed out, and the shepherd had to go ahead and lead his flock into the right paths.

First Child: Yea, though I walk through the valley of the shadow of death, I will fear no evil: for thou art with me; thy rod and thy staff they comfort me.

Second Child: Often the paths went through dark, narrow ravines, where wild animals or thieves might be lurking. The good shepherd went before the sheep to find the way. He helped them with his staff when they got caught in the crags. He used his rod to fight off wild animals.

First Child: Thou preparest a table before me in the presence of mine enemies.

Second Child: Before the shepherd would allow the sheep to graze, he struck the ground with his staff to make sure there were no snakes in the grass. He looked for and destroyed poisonous weeds.

First Child: Thou anointest my head with oil; my cup runneth over.

Second Child: When the day was over, the shepherd examined each sheep to make sure it was not bruised or hurt. If a sheep was scratched and bleeding, the shepherd would rub the wounds with oil.

First Child: Surely goodness and mercy shall follow me all the days of my life: and I will dwell in the house of the Lord for ever.

Second Child: Even after the sheep had been led to the fold, the shepherd did not desert them. He guarded the entrance of the fold through the long night.[1]

[1] From *Child Guidance in Christian Living.* Used by permission.

THE LORD'S PRAYER

Matt. 6:9-13

Father: The followers of Jesus must have often marveled at his strength in the face of hard tasks; his loving concern for everyone who needed and wanted his help; his teachings which were true and bold, yet loving and kind; his life, which showed them what God was like. They knew that one secret of his power was prayer. They wanted to be strong, fearless, and loving, too. So one day they came to him and said, "Master, teach us to pray." Jesus answered them by praying the prayer which we call "The Lord's Prayer." It is a pattern of what a worthy prayer should be. Let us think it through together.

Mother: Our Father

Father: Jesus called God "Father," for he wanted to remind men of God's loving concern for them. He said, not "my Father," but "our Father." God is the Father of all men, and they are brothers of one another.

Mother: Who art in heaven,

Father: Jesus taught us to compare God with the best that we know and then to realize that God is greater than our words can describe.

Mother: Hallowed be thy name.

Father: What does it mean to feel reverent when we think of God? It means the wonder we sense when we look at a sunset sky, or at a hundred snow crystals on a winter day, and realize that God made each one with a pattern all its own. It means the happy stillness that we feel in a quiet church. It means the love we feel when we think of the thoughtful care of our parents. We "hallow" his name when our thoughts of him are high and we earnestly try to live his way.

Mother: Thy kingdom come, thy will be done on earth as it is in heaven.

Father: Jesus helped men see what life would be like when all men learn to live as loving children of God, according to his pattern for their lives. We ought to pray each day: "Thy kingdom come— beginning in me; thy will be done—especially by me."

Mother: Give us this day our daily bread;

Father: The men who listened to Jesus knew what it meant to be hungry. Jesus realized that they could not think of God's way of right living if their minds were full of worry about food. He taught them to pray for food, but he said, "Do not worry about food and clothes. God who is your Father knows you need those things."

Mother: And forgive us our debts, as we also have forgiven our debtors;

Father: Jesus helped men understand what God expects of them. He expects us to right the wrongs we do, and he expects us to give up any feeling of resentment or any grudge we have when someone wrongs us. Only if we forgive those who wrong us is God able to forgive the wrongs we do toward others.

Mother: And lead us not into temptation. But deliver us from evil.

Father: The prayer does not mean that God leads us into evil. It means that if we are tried by evil or attracted to something wrong, we seek God's guidance in making the right choices.

Mother: For thine is the kingdom and the power and the glory, forever. Amen.

Father: This is the chorus of a great song of praise which David, the Hebrew king, once sang. God's rule or reign can come in all its power and beauty when men rightly learn to pray and live Christ's prayer. Let us pray together the prayer.

THE BEATITUDES

Matt. 5:3-11

Father: When Jesus spoke to his closest followers about the way they should live, he began with a list of ways of living which would bring happiness. We call them the "beatitudes," which means the "way of blessedness" or the "way of happiness." They are found at the beginning of Christ's Sermon on the Mount. Let us read them together, pausing after each statement for a sentence which Mother will read to explain its meaning.

All: Blessed are the poor in spirit, for theirs is the kingdom of heaven.

Mother (*or Father*) : Happy are those who feel poor when they think of God's goodness, for they will grow in God's way.

All: Blessed are those who mourn, for they shall be comforted.

Mother: Happy are those who feel sorrow, for God will give them strength and hope.

All: Blessed are the meek, for they shall inherit the earth.

Mother: Happy are those who are patient and humble, for they will possess God's earth.

All: Blessed are those who hunger and thirst for righteousness, for they shall be satisfied.

Mother: Happy are those who feel hungry for goodness and God's way, they shall find them.

All: Blessed are the merciful, for they shall obtain mercy.

Mother: Happy are those who show lovingkindness toward others, for others will treat them with love and understanding also.

All: Blessed are the pure in heart, for they shall see God.

Mother: Happy are those who have pure thoughts and clean habits, for they will find God.

All: Blessed are the peacemakers, for they shall be called sons of God.

Mother: Happy are those who help others live happily together, for they live like true children of God.

All: Blessed are those who are persecuted for righteousness' sake, for theirs is the kingdom of heaven.

Mother: Happy are those who go through trouble and suffering for the sake of goodness, for they will grow in God's way.

A PARALLEL GOSPEL

LIFE OF JESUS

MATTHEW	MARK	LUKE	JOHN

Stories of Jesus' Birth and Boyhood

MATTHEW	MARK	LUKE	JOHN
Coming of the Wise Men 2:1-12		Coming of the Shepherds 2:1-20	
Flight into Egypt 2:13-15			
Return to Nazareth 2:19-23		2:29 Visit to the Temple 2:41-52	

The Baptism of Jesus

MATTHEW	MARK	LUKE	JOHN
3:13-17	1:9-11	3:21-22	1:29-34

The Temptations of Jesus

MATTHEW	MARK	LUKE	JOHN
4:1-11	1:12, 13	4:1-13	

Choosing His Disciples

MATTHEW	MARK	LUKE	JOHN
4:18-22	3:16-20	5:1-11	1:35-51
9:9-17	2:13-22	5:27-32	
10:1-4	3:14-19	6:13-16	

Jesus, the Great Physician

MATTHEW	MARK	LUKE	JOHN
Healing of Peter's Wife's Mother and Others 4:23-25	1:29-34	4:28-44	
Healing the Leper 8:2-4	1:40-45	5:12-16	

MATTHEW	MARK	LUKE	JOHN
Healing the Demoniac of Gadara			
8:28-34	5:1-20	8:26-29	
Healing of Jairus' Daughter			
9:18-26	5:22-40	8:41-56	
Healing of the Paralytic			
9:2-8	2:1-12	5:18-26	
Healing the Man with the Withered Hand on the Sabbath			
12:9-21	3:1-16	6:6-11	

The Teachings of Jesus

MATTHEW	MARK	LUKE	JOHN
The Sermon on the Mount		6:20-49	
5, 6, 7		12:1-34	
Conversation with the Rich Young Ruler			
19:16-23	10:17-31	18:24	
Jesus and the Little Children			
19:13-15	10:13-16	18:15-17	
Anointing in the House of Simon			
26:6-13	14:3-9		12:1-8
Saving Life and Losing It			
16:21-26	9:33-37	9:22-25	
Conversation About Humility			
18:1-5	9:33-37	9:46-48	

The Parables of Jesus
(those recorded in more than one Gospel)

MATTHEW	MARK	LUKE	JOHN
Stories of the New and Old:			
9:16-17	2:21-22	5:36-39	

MATTHEW	MARK	LUKE	JOHN
"The Kingdom Is Like"—			
13:31-48	4:26-32	13:18-21	
The Seed and the Soils			
13:3-9	4:2-8	8:4-8	
13:18-23	4:13-20	8:11-15	
The Wise and Foolish Builders			
7:24-29		6:46-49	
The Empty House			
12:43-45		11:24-26	
The Lost Sheep			
18:12-14		15:1-7	
The Cruel Vinedressers			
21:33-41	12:1-9	20:9-16	
The Rejected Cornerstone			
21:42-45	12:10-11	20:17-18	
The Talents			
25:14-30		19:11-27	

The Passion Week of Jesus' Life

MATTHEW	MARK	LUKE	JOHN
Entry into Jerusalem			
21:1-11	11:1-10	19:29-44	12:12-19
Cleansing of the Temple			
21:12-17	11:15-19	19:45-48	2:13-22
The Widow's Mite			
	12:41-44	21:1-4	
Session of Sanhedrin and Betrayal Compact with Judas			
26:3-5, 14-16	14:1-2, 10-11	22:1-6	
Last Supper			
26:17-30	14:12-26	22:7-34	13:1-14:16
In the Garden			
26:37-45	14:33-41	22:39-46	17:1-18:1

MATTHEW	MARK	LUKE	JOHN
Betrayal of Judas and Arrest of Jesus 26:47-56	14:43-50	22:47-51	18:2-10
Trials of Jesus 26:47–27:26	14:53-15:15	22:54-23:25	18:15-19:16
Crucifixion 27:32-60	5:21-46	23:26-53	19:18-42
Resurrection 28:1-9	16:1-10	24:1-12	20:1-17
Appearances of Jesus After Death to His Followers 28:16-20	16:12, 14	24:13-53	20:19-21:24

HYMN STUDY

Hymns That Paraphrase Scripture Passages

AS PANTS THE HART FOR COOLING STREAMS	Ps. 42
FIGHT THE GOOD FIGHT	II Tim. 4:7-9
HOW LOVELY IS THY DWELLING PLACE	Ps. 84
JESUS SHALL REIGN WHERE'ER THE SUN	Ps. 72
JOY TO THE WORLD!	Ps. 98
O GOD, OUR HELP IN AGES PAST	Ps. 90
O LORD, OUR FATHERS OFT HAVE TOLD	Ps. 44
O MY SOUL, BLESS GOD, THE FATHER	Ps. 103
PRAISE, MY SOUL, THE KING OF HEAVEN	Ps. 103
THE HEAVENS DECLARE THY GLORY	Ps. 19:1-6
THE KING OF LOVE MY SHEPHERD IS	Ps. 23
THE LORD'S MY SHEPHERD	Ps. 23
THE MAN WHO ONCE HAS FOUND ABODE	Ps. 91
THE SPACIOUS FIRMAMENT ON HIGH	Ps. 19:1-6
THROUGH ALL THE CHANGING SCENES OF LIFE	Ps. 34
WALK IN THE LIGHT!	I John 1:7-10
WHILE SHEPHERDS WATCHED THEIR FLOCKS	Luke 2:8-16

HYMNS FOR FAMILY USE

The hymns in these lists have been selected from *The Gospel in Hymns,* by Albert Bailey, rather than from the hymnal of any single denomination. Bailey's studies included those hymns that were found in at least six out of ten widely accepted church hymnals.

Children's Hymns

ALL BEAUTIFUL THE MARCH OF DAYS	AWAY IN A MANGER
ALL CREATURES OF OUR GOD AND KING	COME, YE THANKFUL PEOPLE COME
ALL MY HEART THIS NIGHT REJOICES	
ALL PEOPLE THAT ON EARTH DO DWELL	DAY IS DYING IN THE WEST
ALL THINGS BRIGHT AND BEAUTIFUL	FAIREST LORD JESUS
	FAITH OF OUR FATHERS, LIVING STILL

Father in Heaven Who Lovest All

For the Beauty of the Earth

Forward Be Our Watchword

God That Madest Earth and Heaven

Good Christian Men, Rejoice

Gracious Spirit, Dwell With Me

I Think When I Read That Sweet Story of Old

It Came Upon the Midnight Clear

Joy to the World! The Lord Is Come

Joyful, Joyful We Adore Thee

Let All the World in Every Corner Sing

Let Us With a Gladsome Mind

My Country 'Tis of Thee

My God, I Thank Thee Who Hast Made

Now Thank We All Our God

Now the Day Is Over

O Beautiful for Spacious Skies

O Brother Man, Fold to Thy Heart Thy Brother

O Come, All Ye Faithful

O Little Town of Bethlehem

O Lord of Heaven and Earth and Sea

O Master, Let Me Walk With Thee

O Master Workman of the Race

O Son of Man, Our Hero Strong

Once in Royal David's City

O God, Our Help in Ages Past

Rejoice, Ye Pure in Heart

Saviour, Teach Me Day By Day

Shepherd of Tender Youth

Silent Night

The First Noel

The God of Abraham Praise

The Lord's My Shepherd

The Wise May Bring Their Learning

This Is My Father's World

We Gather Together

We Give Thee But Thine Own

We Plow the Fields and Scatter

What a Friend We Have in Jesus

When Morning Gilds the Skies

While Shepherds Watched Their Flocks

Youth Hymns

A Mighty Fortress Is Our God

Abide with Me

As with Gladness Men of Old

Awake, My Soul, Stretch Every Nerve

O Love That Wilt Not Let Me Go

Once to Every Man and Nation

Ring Out, Wild Bells
Rise Up, O Men of God

Saviour, Breathe an Evening Blessing
Softly Now the Light of Day
Spirit of God, Descend Upon My Heart
Still, Still With Thee

Take My Life, and Let It Be

The Day Thou Gavest, Lord, Is Ended

The Spacious Firmament on High

There's a Wideness in God's Mercy

These Things Shall Be: A Loftier Race

Where Cross the Crowded Ways of Life

A WORSHIP SERVICE ON A PICTURE STUDY

One evening our family was looking at Zimmermann's "Christ and the Fisherman." We had just read from the Gospel of Mark the story of the calling of James and John.

"The old man must be the father," one of the children said.

"Jesus doesn't seem very much interested in James or John. He's just paying attention to Zebedee," remarked another.

"I think it's because he's trying to persuade the father to let his sons become his followers," the first child said.

"How do you think Zebedee feels about letting his boys go?" asked one of the adults in the circle.

"He's wondering what he's going to do for fishermen if his boys leave."

"I'll bet he's wondering just why a great teacher like Jesus would need his boys," said the older boy.

"Jesus is telling him why," the first-grader put in.

"See how Jesus is holding his arm and looking so earnestly at him," the twelve-year-old remarked.

"What I like best in the picture," Mother put in, "is the loving, patient look on the Master's face. As if he really wants Zebedee to know the wonderful way of life he's found, too."

"Do you know what I think he's saying to Zebedee?" asked the youngest child. "I think he's saying, 'Don't worry, Zebedee. God will take care of you.'"

After our circle of prayers that evening we sang with new meaning the prayer response to the melody of Brahms's "Lullaby":

> Saviour, hear us, we pray:
> Keep us safe through this day;
> Keep our lives free from sin
> And our hearts pure within.
>
> Be our Guardian and Guide;
> May we walk by Thy side
> Till the evening shades fall
> Over us—over all.
>
> Jesus, Lord, hear our prayer:
> May we rest in Thy care;
> Jesus, Lord, hear our prayer:
> May we rest in Thy care. Amen.

NATURE STUDY

Scripture Illustrated by Home Photography

The Loving-kindness of the Day

Thine is the day, thine also the night;	*Lakeshore at twilight*
thou hast established the luminaries and the sun.	*Moonlight or sunset over lake*
Thou hast fixed all the bounds of the earth;	*Mountain peak*
thou hast made summer and winter.	*Winter snow scene*
Thou didst cleave open springs and brooks;	*Mountain stream in autumn*
thou didst dry up ever-flowing streams.	*Waterfalls*

—Ps. 74:16-17, 15

The heavens are telling the glory of God;	*Autumn trees against the sky*
and the firmament proclaims his handiwork.	*Vista of woods and sky*
Day by day pours forth speech,	*Sunlight on lakeshore*
and night to night declares knowledge.	*Late sunset over lake*
There is no speech, nor are there words; their voice is not heard;	*Vista from hilltop*
yet their voice goes out through all the earth, and their words to the end of the world.	

—Ps. 19:1-4

By day the Lord commands his steadfast love; and at night this song is with me, a prayer to the God of my life.	*Children on bluff* *Sunset over lake*

—Ps. 42:8

This is the day which the Lord has made;	*Garden in full bloom*
let us rejoice and be glad in it.	*Happy family picture*

.   .   .   .

O Lord how manifold are thy works!
  In wisdom hast thou made them all;
  the earth is full of thy creatures.
Yonder is the sea, great and wide,
  which teems with things innumerable,
  living things both small and great.
	*Palisade bluffs with
	  lake beyond
	Raccoons playing
	View of Pacific
	  Ocean*

These all look to thee, to give them their food in due season.	*Elk feeding*

Thou makest springs gush forth in the valleys;
  they flow between the hills,
By them the birds of the air have their habitation;
  they sing among the branches.
	Cascade waterfalls
	
	*Boys looking into
	bird's nest*

When thou sendest forth thy Spirit, they are
  created;
  and thou renewest the face of the ground.
	Spring wild flowers

From thy lofty abode thou waterest the mountains;
  the earth is satisfied with the fruit of thy work.
    —Ps. 104:24, 25, 27, 10, 12, 30, 13
	*Mountain with snow
	  peak
	Orchard in full fruit*

O give thanks to the Lord, for he is good;
  for his steadfast love endures for ever.
    —Ps. 118:24, 29
	*Church spire or
	  choir*

OTHER NATURE PASSAGES

Ps. 42:1-2; 89:11-15; 23; 65:9-13; Job 38:22, 29, 30, 38; 37:10-16; 36:25-27; Isa. 35:1-2.

NATURE HYMNS TO ILLUSTRATE WITH PICTURES

ALL THINGS BRIGHT AND BEAUTIFUL
THIS IS MY FATHER'S WORLD
GOD, WHO TOUCHEST EARTH WITH BEAUTY
FOR THE BEAUTY OF THE EARTH
ALL CREATURES OF OUR GOD AND KING
O BEAUTIFUL FOR SPACIOUS SKIES
GOD OF THE EARTH, THE SKY, THE SEA
ALL BEAUTIFUL THE MARCH OF DAYS

A FAMILY'S NEW YEAR'S SERVICE

Here is a formal service for the moments following the New Year's breakfast or dinner:

PRELUDE OF HYMN RECORDINGS (perhaps played quietly during the meal)

READING: "The Salutation of Dawn"

> Listen to the Exhortation of the Dawn!
> Look to this Day!
> For it is Life, the very Life of Life.
> In its brief course lie all the
> Verities and realities of your Existence;
>   The Bliss of Growth,
>   The Glory of Action,
>   The Splendor of Beauty;
> For Yesterday is but a Dream,
> And Tomorrow is only a Vision;
> But Today well lived makes
> Every yesterday a Dream of Happiness,
> And every tomorrow a Vision of Hope.
> Look well therefore to this Day!
> Such is the Salutation of the Dawn.
> 　　　　　　　—From the Sanskrit

SING OR READ TOGETHER: "O God, Our Help in Ages Past"

SCRIPTURE: Matt. 6:25-34 (in a modern-speech translation)

CIRCLE OF PLEDGES: What I want to do to make others happy during the coming year

PRAYER OF DEDICATION: Dear Father, as we enter upon this new year, we praise thee for the blessings that have filled the past, and we seek thy guidance upon the future. Give us strength for the work of each day; give us faith for the shadowed hours; give us hope in each new dawn, and renewing rest in the eventide. Grant us the blessings of thy peace, as we walk the way with thee. Amen.

CLOSING PRAYER HYMN: "O Master, Let Me Walk with Thee" (may be read or sung).

THANKSGIVING IN THE FAMILY

Thanksgiving Place-Card Scripture Sentences

O Lord, our Lord,
    how majestic is thy name in all the earth!
                    —Ps. 8:1

I will give thanks to the Lord with my whole heart;
I will tell of all thy wonderful deeds.
                    —Ps. 9:1

O Lord my God, I will give thanks to thee for ever.
                    —Ps. 30:12

I will bless the Lord at all times;
    his praise shall continually be in my mouth.
                    —Ps. 34:1

O Lord, open thou my lips,
    and my mouth shall show forth thy praise.
                    —Ps. 51:15

It is good to give thanks to the Lord,
    to sing praises to thy name, O Most High.
                    —Ps. 92:1

O give thanks to the Lord, call on his name,
    make known his deeds among the peoples!
                    —Ps. 105:1

Praise the Lord!
O give thanks to the Lord, for he is good;
    for his steadfast love endures for ever!
                    —Ps. 106:1

Surely the righteous shall give thanks to thy name;
    the upright shall dwell in thy presence.
                    —Ps. 140:13

A RESPONSIVE THANKSGIVING PRAYER

Prepared by a Family with Small Children

For the beauty of flowers that bloom in the sunshine,
    We give thanks to thee, O God.
For trees and grass, animals and water,
    We give thanks to thee, O God.
For food and drink from thy green world,
    We give thanks to thee, O God.
For Bibles and churches that teach us of thee,
    We give thanks to thee, O God.
For hours and days, and clocks that tell time,
    We give thanks to thee, O God.
For parents and homes where we share and love,
    We give thanks to thee, O God.

EVENING PRAYER

Lord, the evening hour has come,
And we pause within our home
Thanking Thee for blessings here
    And for Thy beauties everywhere
    That bring us joy.

Holy, Holy, Holy, Father of all,
    Happy hearts and loving ways
Help us all to tell Thy praise
    Through every day. Amen.[1]

[1] Tune: "Day Is Dying in the West."

SERVICE OF HOME DEDICATION

PRELUDE OF INSTRUMENTAL OR RECORDED MUSIC: "Faith of Our Fathers!" "Joyful, Joyful, We Adore Thee"

FATHER: We have paused after the tasks of the week for this quiet hour to give thanks for our new home and to seek God's blessing as we begin our living within its walls.

FAMILY HYMN: (May be sung by the family, as a solo by one member, or read by the mother)

> Happy the home when God is there,
> And love fills every breast;
> When one their wish, and one their prayer,
> And one their heavenly rest.
>
> Happy the home where Jesus' name
> Is sweet to every ear;
> Where children early lisp his fame,
> And parents hold him dear.
>
> Happy the home where prayer is heard,
> And praise is wont to rise;
> Where parents love the sacred Word,
> And all its wisdom prize.
>
> Lord, let us in our homes agree
> This blessed peace to gain;
> Unite our hearts in love to thee
> And love to all will reign.[1]
>
> —Henry Ware, Jr.

CHORIC READING: "The Parable of the Builders" (see p. 138 for arrangement)

SIMPLE STORY OR FAMILY DISCUSSION: "How a House Becomes a Home" (If the family is alone, discuss the differences between a house and a home, and ask each person to suggest something he can do to make the new house a real home.)

SCRIPTURE READING: I Cor. 13 (by the mother or by the family. See p. 140 for choric-reading arrangement.)

[1] Tune: "St. Agnes."

PRAYER OF DEDICATION

Father and Family

All: Dear Father, already the work of our hands has hallowed the walls of our home. Help us remember that the work we do happily for one another, we do for thee.

Family: We dedicate this home to work.

Father: Our play unites us, God, and teaches us to forget ourselves in our enjoyment of one another. Make all our play clean, wholesome, and glad.

Family: We dedicate this home to play.

Father: Open wide the doors of our home to friends and strangers, Father. May they find here refreshment for body and spirit.

Family: We dedicate this home to friendship.

Father: Help us remember, Father, that Christ came to serve and that he lives in our deeds of service to others.

Family: We dedicate this home to service.

Father: In love was our family born, our Father. By love we are nurtured and sustained. In love we would live with one another. Through love we find our surest path to thee.

Family: We dedicate this home to love.

BENEDICTION: By father or minister

BENEDICTIONS FOR FAMILY USE

The Lord bless you and keep you:
The Lord make his face to shine upon
you, and be gracious to you:
The Lord lift up his countenance upon
you, and give you peace. Amen.
—Num. 6:24-26

May the Lord make [our] love for one another and for all men wide and full . . . so that [our] hearts may be strong and faultlessly pure. Amen.— I Thess. 3:12 (Goodspeed)

May Christ dwell in [our] hearts through faith, that [we], being rooted and grounded in love, . . . may be filled with the fullness of God. Amen. —Eph. 3:17-19

The peace of God, which passeth understanding, keep your hearts and minds in the love and knowledge of God and of his Son, Jesus Christ, our Lord. Amen.

A MOTTO FOR THE HOME

Christ is the Head of this house,
The Unseen Guest at every meal,
The Silent Listener to every conversation.

BIRTHDAY GREETINGS FROM THE BIBLE

The Lord bless you and keep you.

—Num. 6:24

The God of peace shall be with you.

—Phil. 4:9

The peace of God, which passeth understanding, shall keep your hearts and minds through Christ Jesus.

—Phil. 4:7

Jesus said, "Lo, I am with you alway."

—Matt. 28:20

The Lord make you to increase and abound in love one toward another, and toward all men, even as we do toward you.

—I Thess. 3:12

Jesus said, "Blessed are the pure in heart; for they shall see God."

—Matt. 5:8

A BIRTHDAY PRAYER FOR A CHILD

Dear Father, today is ———'s birthday. He has brought happiness to us every day since he was born. We remember the joy his coming brought. We are glad that he belongs to us. We thank thee for his loving, happy ways. We thank thee that he is well and strong, and has an eager, growing mind.

Today our prayer is especially for him. Help him grow as Jesus grew "in wisdom and in stature, and in favor with God and man." May he continue to bring joy to others. May he find happy ways of showing his love for thee, for his family, and for his friends. May he find love and kindness in everyone he meets, and may he continue to discover evidences of thy care in everything about him.

As we join in wishing him a happy birthday, we pledge to him and to thee our loving care for him and for all thy other children. Amen.

WORSHIP HELP IN TIMES OF NEED

WHEN THE FAMILY FACES EXPERIENCES THAT CALL FOR DEDICATION TO GOD'S WAY

1. Moving into a new community
   SCRIPTURE: Ps. 127:1; Matt. 7:24-28; I Cor. 1:3; Col. 3; Prov. 16:17
   HYMNS: "O God, Our Help in Ages Past"; "O Happy Home, Where Thou Art Loved"

2. At the birth of a child
   SCRIPTURE: Luke 2:1-20; Matt. 18:1-6
   HYMNS: "Saviour, Teach Me, Day by Day"; "Lord of Life and King of Glory"; "Shepherd of Tender Youth"

3. When beginning new work
   SCRIPTURE: Phil. 3:12-17; 2:13
   HYMNS: "O Master, Let Me Walk with Thee"; "Forth in Thy Name, O Lord, I Go"; "Fight the Good Fight"

4. When a member of the family joins the church
   SCRIPTURE: John 3:1-21; Luke 10:25-28; Rom. 12
   HYMNS: "He Who Would Valiant Be"; "Spirit of Life, in This New Dawn"; "O Young and Fearless Prophet"

5. When an older son or daughter establishes a new home
   SCRIPTURE: I Cor. 13; Gen. 29:1-20; Ruth 1:16-18; Prov. 31:10-31
   HYMNS: "O Love Divine and Golden"; "O Perfect Love"

WHEN OUR FAITH IN THE CHRISTIAN WAY IS TESTED

1. When resentments and misunderstandings separate us from others
   SCRIPTURE: Matt. 5:43-48; Matt. 7:12; Luke 6:35-38; Eph. 4:31-32
   HYMNS: "There's a Wideness in God's Mercy"; "Blest Be the Tie That Binds"; "Breathe on Me, Breath of God"

2. When we have been wronged and are trying to forgive
   SCRIPTURE: Philemon; Matt. 18:21-35; 6:14-15; Gal. 6:1-10
   HYMNS: "Dear Lord and Father of Mankind"; "Dear God, Our Father, at Thy Knee Confessing"; "Draw Thou My Soul, O Christ."

3. When we face a moral decision
   SCRIPTURE: Matt. 4:1-17; Eph. 3:14-21; James 1:12-23
   HYMNS: "Lead Us, O Father, in the Paths of Peace"; "I Want a Principle Within"

4. When we are faced with a task that seems too great for us

SCRIPTURE: Matt. 5:13-16; 7:7-11; Eph. 6:10-18; Phil. 4:11-13
HYMNS: "Be Strong"; 'Courage, Brother! Do Not Stumble;" "Jesus, Kneel Beside Me"

WHEN THE FAMILY FACES EXPERIENCES OF INSECURITY

1. In times of financial tension
   SCRIPTURE: Matt. 6:7-13; 6:19-34
   HYMNS: "Lord, For Tomorrow and Its Needs"; "This Is My Father's World"

2. When a member of the family is seriously ill
   SCRIPTURE: Ps. 67; Isa. 26:3-4; 40:28-31
   HYMNS: "Spirit of God, Descend upon My Heart"; "If, on a Quiet Sea"; "We May Not Climb the Heavenly Steeps"

3. When natural dangers threaten
   SCRIPTURE: Ps. 90:1-6, 14-17; 91; II Tim. 1:12
   HYMNS: "Strong Son of God, Immortal Love"; "God Moves in a Mysterious Way"; "Be Still, My Soul"; "O God, Our Help in Ages Past"

4. In times of community or national tension
   SCRIPTURE: Mic. 4:2-5; 6:8; Amos 5:21-24; Jer. 22:13-16; Ps. 100
   HYMNS: "God of Grace and God of Glory"; "O Gracious Father of Mankind"; "That Cause Can Neither Be Lost Nor Stayed"

WHEN THE FAMILY FACES SEPARATION

1. When parents are separated from each other or from their children
   SCRIPTURE: John 15:1-14; Eph. 4:1-7, 11-16; 6:10-18
   HYMNS: "Father, Lead Me Day by Day"; "Saviour, Like a Shepherd Lead Us"

2. When a son or daughter leaves for school
   SCRIPTURE: Col. 3:12-17; James 1:2-8; II Tim. 2:15; Ps. 119; Prov. 3:13-24; 4:5-9
   HYMNS: "O Master Workman of the Race"; "O Thou Whose Feet Have Climbed Life's Hill"; "Faith of Our Fathers!"

3. When the family circle is broken by death
   SCRIPTURE: Ps. 23; John 14; Heb. 11:1-3, 13-16; Matt. 28:20
   HYMNS: "In Heavenly Love Abiding"; "I Know Not What the Future Hath"

BIBLIOGRAPHY

GUIDING RELIGIOUS GROWTH IN THE FAMILY

Hamilton, Mrs. Clarence H. *Doorways to a Happy Home.* Indianapolis: The Bobbs-Merrill Company, Inc., 1950.
————. *Our Children and God.* Indianapolis: The Bobbs-Merrill Company, Inc., 1952.
Jones, Mary Alice. *The Faith of Our Children.* New York and Nashville: Abingdon-Cokesbury Press, 1943.
Maynard, Donald M. *Your Home Can Be Christian.* New York and Nashville: Abingdon-Cokesbury Press, 1952.
Odell, Mary Clemens. *Our Family Grows Toward God.* New York and Nashville: Abingdon-Cokesbury Press, 1949.
Staples, Ethelyne and Edward. *Children in a Christian Home.* New York and Nashville: Abingdon-Cokesbury Press, 1948.
Wood, Leland Foster. *Growing Together in the Family.* New York and Nashville: Abingdon-Cokesbury Press, 1935.

TECHNIQUES FOR FAMILY WORSHIP

Black, Guy, Oliver, and Ira. *How to Conduct Family Worship at the Table.* Nashville: Upper Room Press, 1949 (rev.) .
Ferre, Nels F. S. *Strengthening the Spiritual Life.* New York: Harper & Brothers, 1951. See chap. "Strengthening Through Family Devotions."
Gebhard, Anna Laura. *Parsonage Doorway.* New York and Nashville: Abingdon-Cokesbury Press, 1950. See chap. "Sanctuary Hours."
McGavran, Grace W. *And When You Pray.* Boston: Pilgrim Press, 1941.
Thomas, Mazelle Wildes. *The Family Worships Together.* Boston: Pilgrim Press, 1949.

RESOURCES FOR FAMILY WORSHIP

Prayers

Clough, William A. *Father, We Thank Thee.* New York and Nashville: Abingdon-Cokesbury Press, 1949. Two hundred graces and one hundred prayers for the home, simply phrased.

Hamilton, Mrs. Clarence H. *God Lives in Homes.* St. Louis: Bethany Press, 1942.

Let Us Give Thanks. Boston: Pilgrim Press, n.d. A file of family prayers and graces.

Moore, Jessie Eleanor. *Children's Prayers for Every Day.* New York & Nashville: Abingdon-Cokesbury Press, 1949.

Taylor, Florence M. *Thine Is the Glory.* Philadelphia: Westminster Press, 1948. Stories that interpret the Lord's Prayer to children.

The Book of Worship for Church and Home. Nashville: Methodist Publishing House, 1944.

The Family Looks at One World. Boston: Pilgrim Press, 1950. Thoughts and prayers for family worship.

UNDERSTANDING AND USING THE BIBLE

Abingdon Bible Commentary. New York and Nashville: Abingdon-Cokesbury Press, 1929.

Bowie, Walter Russell. *The Bible Story for Boys and Girls (Old Testament).* New York and Nashville: Abingdon-Cokesbury Press, 1952.

————. *The Bible Story for Boys and Girls (New Testament).* New York and Nashville: Abingdon-Cokesbury Press, 1951.

————. *The Story of the Bible.* New York and Nashville: Abingdon-Cokesbury Press, 1934.

By an Unknown Disciple. New York: Harper & Brothers, 1919.

Entwistle, Mary. *The Bible Guidebook.* New York and Nashville: Abingdon-Cokesbury Press, 1936.

Gebhard, Anna Laura. *Enjoying the Bible at Home.* St. Louis: Bethany Press, 1951.

Goodspeed, Edgar. *The Story of the Bible.* Chicago: University of Chicago Press.

Jones, Mary Alice. *His Name Was Jesus.* Chicago: Rand McNally & Co., 1950.

Miller, Madeline and J. Lane. *Encyclopedia of Bible Life.* New York: Harper & Brothers.

Tubby, Ruth. *Picture Dictionary of the Bible.* New York and Nashville: Abingdon-Cokesbury Press, 1949.

The Westminster Historical Atlas to the Bible. Philadelphia: Westminster Press, 1946.

RELIGIOUS MUSIC AND ART

Bailey, Albert. *The Gospel in Art.* Boston: Pilgrim Press, 1936.

————. *The Gospel in Hymns.* New York: Charles Scribner's Sons, 1950.

Brown, Jeanette Perkins. *A Little Book of Singing Graces.* New York and Nashville: Abingdon-Cokesbury Press, 1946.

————. *A Little Book of Bedtime Songs.* New York and Nashville: Abingdon-Cokesbury Press, 1947.

In Joyous Song. A set of hymn recordings for little children.

Smith, H. Augustine. *Lyric Religion.* New York: Fleming H. Revell Co., 1931.

SOURCES FOR PREPARED FAMILY DEVOTIONS

Niedermeyer, Mabel. *Sometime Every Day*. St. Louis: Christian Board of Education, 1948. Everyday incidents and problems. Scripture, prayers, poems.

Staples, Edward (comp.). *Prayertime*. Nashville: Upper Room Press, 1952.

Welker-Barber. *Thoughts of God for Boys and Girls*. New York: Harper & Brothers, 1948.

QUARTERLIES

The Secret Place. Philadelphia: American Baptist Publishing Society.

Power. Nashville: For youth. National Conference, Methodist Youth Fellowship.

Thoughts of God for Boys and Girls. Connecticut Council of Churches.

Today. Philadelphia: Westminster Press.

Upper Room. Nashville: Upper Room Press.

MAGAZINES WITH FAMILY DEVOTIONS

Hearthstone. St. Louis: Christian Board of Publication.

The Christian Home. Nashville: Methodist Publishing House.

INDEX